Roller Derby Art

Women, Wheels, and Wicked Fun

Sherri Cullison Pfouts

4880 Lower Valley Road Atglen, Pennsylvania 19310

Dedication

In Memory of Tyrone "Buck" Cullison

Schiffer Books are available at special discounts for bulk purchases for sales promotions or premiums. Special editions, including personalized covers, corporate imprints, and excerpts can be created in large quantities for special needs. For more information contact the publisher:

Published by Schiffer Publishing Ltd.
4880 Lower Valley Road
Atglen, PA 19310
Phone: (610) 593-1777; Fax: (610) 593-2002
E-mail: Info@schifferbooks.com

For the largest selection of fine reference books on this and related subjects, please visit our web site at
www.schifferbooks.com
We are always looking for people to write books on new and related subjects. If you have an idea for a book please contact us at the above address.

This book may be purchased from the publisher.
Include $5.00 for shipping.
Please try your bookstore first.
You may write for a free catalog.

In Europe, Schiffer books are distributed by
Bushwood Books
6 Marksbury Ave.
Kew Gardens
Surrey TW9 4JF England
Phone: 44 (0) 20 8392-8585; Fax: 44 (0) 20 8392-9876
E-mail: info@bushwoodbooks.co.uk
Website: www.bushwoodbooks.co.uk
Free postage in the U.K., Europe; air mail at cost.

Copyright © 2008 by Sherri Cullison
Library of Congress Control Number: 2008928745

Covers and book designed by: Bruce Waters
Type set in Zurich BT

ISBN: 978-0-7643-3063-6
Printed in China

Acknowledgements

Most assuredly, I will forget someone important in this list, but I'll start by thanking those I love the most, my family (and my biggest fans): Chris Pfouts, Irvin and Geraldine Cullison, Karen, Rick, Brittany and Michelle Keen, Ryan Donovan, Greg, Cathee, Bradley and Lauren Cullison, and Betty and Caroline Pfouts, plus all my many aunts, uncles and cousins who come out to cheer at all the bouts. Thanks also goes to my best of friends: Mandy Marie Luke, Neal Taflinger, Matt Gonzales, Michelle Pemberton and Ben Roe, Traci, Medhane and Miles Cumbay, Amy Young, Deanne Staley, Greg "The Mayor" Andrews, Joey Pichette, and Laura Gharst. To Mark Brocklehurst for not only kicking my ass and getting me in shape, but for being a truly great friend—let the chips (and teeth) fall where they may, Mr. Whip. To Elizabeth Hufnagel and Amber Martin, both for being my best girlfriends and for getting the Naptown Roller Girls going. To each of the members of the Naptown Roller Girls—the skaters (the loveliest partners in crime a girl could have), the fans (the Naptown Roller Girl [unofficial] Fan Club!), the many volunteers, and the refs. And thanks to many more: Jerry Lee's Western Wear, Hodges Massages, the Metamorphosis crew, Amy McAdams, Shauta Marsh, Mandy Marie and the Cool Hand Lukes and the Cool Hand Lukes regulars, DJ Sarah Vain, Uncle Leon and the Alibis, Mark Miller, Roy and Diane Caruthers, Renee Sweany, Nikki Sutton, Tom Klubens, Amanda Rose Mauer, Eric Smith, Brian Popkie, Durb Morrison, Brad and Callie Powers, Dan and Toni Carr, Danny Thompson, The Exiles, The Push-Rods and The Emperors car clubs, Bobby Rothenberger, Jason Pitman, Dale Rio, Athena Barbital, Mitch O'Connell, Frank, White Knuckles, Little Mike, Squeak, and Bunny. Thanks to David Zivan for believing in second chances and for reminding me that writing—good writing—is hard. And, most of all, special thanks to each of the artists and writers who contributed their work and talents to this book.

Look at today's roller derby. It is a volcano unlike any other: A wildly popular wholly independent sport that is international in scope, completely built on grass roots, with only a vague sanctioning body and no big-cheese owners. Although it has a history, it has no precedent. It is unique as a sport, as a structure, and as a social phenomenon. Not only is there no other sport that operates on such a widespread, hog-on-ice basis, but there is no other human endeavor that I can think of that works like roller derby works. There is some kind of Monster Mystery Factor at work among the small wheels.

Alcoholics Anonymous is widespread and independent, like derby, but AA lacks that all-important full-contact angle, and it leaves a lot to be desired as a spectator sport.

In the early 1950s, for a brief period, the sport of drag racing was similar to roller derby today—independent knots of guys around the country were getting together with timing equipment and racing each other on abandoned air strips. But the parallel is not perfect. Honest drag racing requires accurate measurement devices you can verify for accuracy, and a central sanctioning body really helped with that. Plus there was a hoodlum aspect to hotrodding in those days. Drag racers needed good PR to not be seen as thugs on wheels. A central authority gave the sport a legitimate face and tied everyone together.

Tying roller girls together is not the problem. The problem is keeping them apart.

No, this roller derby of today stands alone in a lot of ways. As such, it's something to be admired, treasured and wondered about.

These women huddle up and start their local organizations. There is nobody to cut up territory or divide turf. They can either ask around for counseling and advice on ways and means, hows and whys, or not. They can use coaches, generals, trainers, dictators—or none of the above. Eventually they stand up and say, we're ready to play, and call around for some competition. Then the teams get together and play. And fans flock to watch it. That's a gross oversimplification, but still a fair description of the process. There is the Women's Flat Track Derby Association (WFTDA), which holds itself out as a sanctioning organization, but many teams exist outside WFTDA lines, and many games generate mucho fun without the organization's say-so.

Modern roller derby's most prominent asset is its fun, built on a foundation of enthusiasm and energy. Fans and players have the juice, sure, but you also find it among those doing the grittier necessary jobs: selling and taking tickets, parking cars, minding security, setting up and breaking down venues, and so on. Top to bottom, inside and out, people love roller derby and express that love through work. The bouts are the shiny part of this deal that everyone sees, but in real time and real terms, the bouts are a tiny fraction of the activity involved in roller derby. Like any good show, a lot of hard work goes into making it look easy.

Which brings us back to the Monster Mystery Factor. No traditional risk versus reward, or work and payoff equation will explain the fire that crackles through roller derby. None of the usual volunteer models will do it, either, and the carrot and stick don't apply. There is something here that attracts the best and brightest people, and far more important, squeezes the best and brightest efforts from those who are not generally the best and brightest. People give their all for roller derby up and down the scale, from star jammers and silver-tongued announcers to the guy waltzing the push broom an hour after the bout is over. They give their all, do their best, spiff up and wear a smile, and that dedication holds up over years.

Most employers can't buy that dedication and focus for money. Politicians dream of campaign crews with half that drive and ability. This is where the aspects of derby's uniqueness and Monster Mystery Factor begin to blend into one high-velocity shining icon.

Where the Monster Mystery Factor comes from, I don't know. Where roller derby is going—and believe me, it is going somewhere—I don't know. But I do know that we, as a society, really needed roller derby. We needed it bad, and that ain't good. When it arrived we embraced it like a drowning man muckles onto a floating log.

But we didn't know we needed it. There was a big void there that almost no one could see. I actually think no one at all could see it. I believe this was a thing started for local kicks that has run wild and almost accidentally sprung up gigantic, and equally by accident satisfied an aching national need of which we were not aware. There are legions of hustlers out there looking to find some kind of entertainment gap to fill. They are trying boozy, R-rated, semi-pro female pillow fights, things like that. So far none of them has really hit the switch. Derby did it accidentally. Which makes me wonder, what else is society pining for?

Until that question is answered, we have roller derby, and roller derby has us. I'm one of those people who volunteers for grubby derby-side jobs: doing security, breaking down chairs, constructing sound equipment. I contribute what I can with my talents.

Much of the graphic talent that swirls around the ranks of roller derby is in this book. Consistent with the usual derby style, these poster artists faced no high-hat, Snooty McBooty judges to get in. They presented the fruits of their labor by invitation, or sans invite, with their lances swinging free; underpaid, even unpaid, happy to contribute. Consider these fliers and posters as calls to kicks, the urban equivalent to an island dude blowing into a conch shell.

These are invitations to individual eruptions of the derby volcano. Come get some on you.

Chris Pfouts

Contents

They Spinnin'!
The Wheels of the Sport

Reno, Chicago, Minnesota, Buffalo, Toronto ... Johnny Cash sang it. Hank Snow crooned it before him, and the "it" is a song called "I've Been Everywhere." Roller derby, like Cash and Snow, has been everywhere, man. The sport is traveling the globe—via eight wheels.

A pal recently told me that roller derby was old news—"It's seven years old," he emphatically informed me of the sport's current resurgence. And so I was supposed to agree that derby is used-up, old hat, so yesterday and way last year. My friend doesn't understand. For one, he's yet to attend a bout. I'll do what I can to change that. Then hopefully he'll see.

In Indianapolis, the Naptown Roller Girls (of which I'm a member) bring in approximately 3,000 screaming fans for each bout. Spectators drink beer. They buy T-shirts, calendars, posters, foam fingers, wristbands, beer cozies and butt cushions. Then they line the track with their loot for two or so hours of all-out action—and some seriously frenzied fun. I've heard the roar of screams as we've circled the track—it's mostly all I can hear when I'm skating in a bout. I've signed autographs for fans young and old, preppy, peppy, and high-class, and others not-so. Derby draws a huge mix of fans, and the key word there? Huge.

Renee Sweany wrote an essay for this book about starting the Naptown Roller Girls [unofficial] Fan Club; she (as well as hundreds of others) found herself at an NRG bout and was instantly drawn in. Sweany now manages a Web site (www.nrgfanclub.com) and a mailing list that goes out to fans. Club members have tailgated before bouts; they've created merchandise of their own; they've climbed onto tour buses to follow us on the road.

NRG has gained widespread acceptance in Indy, well-known for being a sports town; as I write, we're six days away from our inaugural bout of the league's second season. People are waiting. They're buying tickets. They're sending us messages of encouragement. They're antsy. Random people have stopped me to say they believe derby is the "best thing going" in Indianapolis. That may or may not be true, it's subjective, after all, but if these people believe it, what's the harm? I've stumbled upon other fans I didn't know I even had. One such instance: Two young boys arrived on my doorstep looking for Halloween night tricks or treats, and they greeted me by name: "Hello, Touretta Lynn."

Touretta Lynn is my alter ego, my name on the track when I'm dressed in red and black as one of fourteen gals competing on Naptown's team, The Tornado Sirens. My skater name and my new sport have brought my family members together for reunions of sorts—to cheer on their girl. I've gained a new family, too—some of the best people I know (all types, all sizes, all classes) skate alongside me.

And there's more. Derby has reunited me with sport—I quit playing softball and basketball in high school. I'm now 35, and I've been skating six or more hours a week for the last two-and-a-half years. Roller derby is a constant challenge. It's time-consuming, it's occasionally frightening, and it's seriously exhausting. Joining a roller derby league has put me in the best shape of my life: my muscles are toned, my endurance reaching stellar.

There are so many reasons to love roller derby. And there are so many more reasons why derby is so now ... not then. I'll get into those later. For now, I will say that roller derby *has* come and gone several times over the past decades. But—despite the old saying—all good things don't really ever have to end. They simply take a tumble—and get back up again.

25¢

1959

ROLLER
DERBY

The skate of champions

OFFICIAL

★ ★

Name and Trade Mark
Reg. U. S. Pat. Office
ROLLER DERBY
SKATE

PRICE:

Roller derby hit the track in the 1930s, though I've read bits and pieces about the sport—or at least the name—dating back to the '20s and before. But most place derby's start during the thick of the Depression, when a fella named Leo Seltzer corralled skaters for The Transcontinental Roller Derby, which was basically a race. Two teams of men and women donned eight wheels and took turns skating nearly 4,000 miles on a track at the Chicago Coliseum. Spectators swarmed, and one of them—famous newspaperman Damon Runyon—later tipped Seltzer, who had by then taken his show on the road, to a better idea: Keep score and encourage scuffles. Fisty-cuffs, after all, make for big fun.

Thus, roller derby—as most have come to know it—was officially born. The banked-track sport became increasingly rough; fans then became increasingly enamored with roller derby.

Television helped derby grow into a nationally known sport during the 1950s; radio broadcasts also aided in spreading the gospel. Around this time many skaters became well-known personalities, and derby's popularity stayed strong for a good number of years, decades even. The Transcontinental derby changed hands and moved, and it wasn't until the '70s—despite Hollywood attention (think "Kansas City Bombers" and Raquel Welch) and attempts by various show promoters to develop it as entertainment—that the sport really started to nosedive. There were various versions of derby and even more Hollywood creations during the last decades of the 20th century—"Roller Jam," a television series, and "Rollerball," a movie that depicts the sport as an ugly metaphor for the emerging corporate world, come to mind. Several other television series, movies, books and derby organizations popped up, too.

But nothing seemed to stick. Throughout the 1970s, derby raged with fights and personal dramas. And spectators became despondent. What had once brought heaving masses in to watch the action had begun to backfire on its creators. Roller derby took on the stigma often associated with the staged fights and rivalries characteristic of the World Wrestling Federation. People stopped believing.

Then, around the year 2000, something happened in Texas. And in Phoenix. And

Los Angeles. And Las Vegas. And Seattle. Female-run roller derby leagues—a few banked-track and, most of them, flat-track—were organizing all over the country. Eventually, they were showing up in Toronto, and in London, and in New Zealand. And later in small towns, too. Despite its short-lived existence on television airwaves, the A&E Network real-life series "Rollergirls" helped to spin roller derby's wheels once again. By the time "Rollergirls" fell to the history books, the idea had taken hold, and this time with a fresh look and spirit.

The leagues were skater-owned and operated with a do-it-yourself attitude. Skaters hit the tracks in fishnet stockings, short skirts and mad make-up. The sport now combined punk-rock aesthetics, pin-up pulchritude, and athletic ability into one showy existence. But there was more behind the curtain. These were big events brought to the masses by entrepreneurial-minded women running businesses while also venturing into a new game. Dale Rio, who skates as "Black Dahlia" and who runs *Blood & Thunder* magazine, which is dedicated solely to the sport, wrote an essay for this book about helping a bunch of girls start a roller derby league in Auckland, New Zealand. She goes into what it took to first find and organize future skaters, and then to market the idea to the public.

I got in on the ground level with the Naptown Roller Girls, a league made up of about 20 or so skaters, one coach, a half-dozen or so referees, and numerous volunteers, so I was able to see—and help tackle—the multitude of tasks that needed to be completed to get the league up and running. The league was named; tax and business forms were filled out. We needed branding and logos, sponsorships from local businesses, a competing team name, membership dues, a code of conduct, and non-compete clauses.

Photographs were taken of our girls, uniforms were made, skating equipment was bought, practice spaces rented, bouts scheduled (which meant finding other teams to play), advertisements sold for our bout programs (programs that also needed designers and writers, mind you), a Web site created, public relations handled, tickets ordered, posters made (and then spanked onto windows and walls throughout the city), and more. Committees were formed and meetings were regularly held for the seemingly endless number of tasks.

As a budding photojournalist, Joe Vitti, who now works full-time as a photographer for the *Indianapolis Star* daily newspaper, caught derby on film at New York's Madison Square Gardens in 1974.

Photo by Joe Vitti.

The late roller derby queen, Ann Calvello, was involved in the sport for most of her life. Photo by Joe Vitti.

There in the gestational stages of NRG, we also all needed to get in shape and learn how to skate. We looked for—and found—girls to go through the rigors of training by our coach, Mark Brocklehurst, who also wrote an essay in this book. Brocklehurst, known to the skaters as Mr. Whip, is tough; many girls have come and gone because they were unable—or unwilling—to keep up with the training schedule. We come together three times a week for two hours each practice. The practices themselves are grueling. And that's an understatement.

We've spent hours running, jumping, lifting, and holding our still bodies in positions designed—I'm certain—only for cruel-and-unusual punishment. We've completed thousands of crunches by now, even more push-ups, tricep push-ups, leg lifts, side-plank dips, and scissor kicks. We've run miles around the rink; we've run miles in place—going nowhere at all; we've climbed up and down stairs; we've attached other skaters to our backs and run—pulling both them and us across the rink. Occasionally a few girls cry, or hyperventilate, or both. Then when we're done with all that, we skate.

There are several reasons we put so much into the athletics part of the equation. One, because of the obvious: It's fun to win, and bouts are tough. We need to be in the best shape possible to last the three all-out periods during which the game is played.

But two, roller derby is a dangerous sport. I'm not going to lie. It's frightening. One of the worst moments for many girls—including myself—is standing on the track and listening to the national anthem. It's the longest and shortest song I've ever heard. Now, hearing it outside of the track incites insta-fear. When the anthem starts before a bout, it means we have approximately two minutes until the start of play, two minutes until the unexpected, two minutes until possible pain.

One gal in Chicago recently fell during a bout and damaged her spine. She's no longer skating, and, in fact, she's no longer walking. That's an extreme case for a derby injury, but extremes do happen. The injury list for our own league continues to grow. We've seen a steady flow of torn tendons, broken ankles, arms, wrists, and tailbones, even toenails falling off; that's not to mention the continual bruises, the aches, the pains, the groans. Derby is dangerous, and the better shape you're in—the better chance you have of making it out safely. That's not to say the only girls who get hurt aren't in great shape. Some things you just can't stop—like physics. We've had girls go sliding into steps, flying into walls, and getting crushed underneath a pile of bodies. Hey, it's roller derby. That's why it's fun to watch, right?

And there's a third reason why training is so important. We respect roller derby for what it is—a sport. Derby is hard; it's physical; it's demanding. We aren't a sideshow act. This is not "Carnival." We don't paint our faces—though some skaters do. And, yes, we may have short skirts and fishnets, but, considering the practices, trips to the gym, membership dues, event coordination, public and charity events, and possible injuries we face, this is serious business. It's damn-near a full-time job.

Tara Armov and Suzy Snakeyes take a tumble in a modern-day bout. Photo by Dale Rio.

The L.A. Derby Dolls wait for the whistle to blow. Photo by Dale Rio.

The Windy City Rollers strategize during a period break. Photo by Dale Rio.

Derby has taken some pretty hard hits throughout the years, and today's version is really no different. When many first hear about our budding league, they immediately liken it to what they know of WWF. They expect fights. They want brawls. They need fists flying and hair being pulled. It's not exactly like that—not always, at least. I *was* punched in the face during one bout. Now, nearly a year later, the skater throwing the punch won't let go of her moment; she keeps the photos of the incident posted on the homepage of her MySpace account like badges of honor. Each to his or her own, I guess; we latch onto our greatest moments of glory any way we can.

But with the Naptown Roller Girls, as with many other leagues, derby isn't about the fights and flash. Derby is the best sport going for women. Yes, tempers do flare, cusswords do fly, but that's all part of succumbing to the heat of a competition. And if occasionally a fight breaks out—bad on the two ladies involved. They get thrown out.

In 2007, the Naptown Roller Girls became members of the Women's Flat Track Derby Association, which is a national governing body for women's amateur flat-track roller derby in the U.S. As a new member of WFTDA, the Naptown Roller Girls join the ranks of approximately 50 all-female, skater-owned and -operated leagues nationwide that have united to lead the growing sport. WFTDA member leagues engage in sanctioned inter-league play, including regional and national tournaments.

There are still many more leagues out there that don't yet belong to WFTDA; in the U.S. alone, nearly 200 leagues are active. Derby leagues have to go through an application process to get in to WFTDA, and, once they're in, they're subject to being thrown out if they don't abide by WFTDA rules

and regulations. One of those rules: sportswomanlike conduct, which translates to no fighting if you're one to read between the lines.

Instead of trackside drama, these WFTDA leagues focus on the athletics. There are training camps for derby taking place all over the country—several of which occur during the annual RollerCon events, which draw thousands, in Las Vegas. All this is to say: Women everywhere are taking derby, with its nasty spills, bruised butts and egos, and point-scoring glory, seriously.

And yet there've been many discussions about whether derby really is a sport, considering the outfits we wear and the pseudonyms we bear. The sports editor at Indy's local newspaper refuses to recognize derby in the sports pages, he says, because we have false names. Ethically, he reasons, he can't provide the coverage without using our real names. I've been cut off in conversation every time I've mentioned the fact that we're willing to have our real names printed. I recognize a losing battle when I see one, and, truthfully, the guy is tops in my book; we get along great, so I refuse to push it too far. Instead, the derby girls have found coverage in the paper's "features" section; we're a novelty act. So sad.

And still other conversations have gone by way of our dress. Detractors proclaim the outfits objectify the ladies involved. Others speak to the empowerment felt when skating in a skirt. I don't really see it either way, and I suppose it's because I like to keep things simple. Short skirts are hella-fun. I used to run clad in miniskirts and thigh-high stockings as a high-school punker. Now, in my mid-30s, I'm outfitting myself in the same gear I thought I'd put to rest forever decades ago. It's a little funny, and it's a refreshing change. So we're wearing fishnets and short skirts; we're still kicking ass.

PENALTY or FAIR PLAY?

ILLEGAL ELBOW BLOCK | LEGAL ELBOW BLOCK

ILLEGAL LEG BLOCK | LEGAL LEG BLOCK

ILLEGAL LOCKING | ILLEGAL SCRAPPING

The Game

To the uninitiated, roller derby might look to be a no-rules race with skaters going all eight-wheeled willy-nilly on one another. As a skater, indeed, I agree it sometimes feels like that. When the ladies are rolling, the fans are screaming, the music's blaring, the coach is yelling, and the announcers are doing their well-seasoned fast-talking, the action blurs into an adrenaline rush of motion and noise; one minute you're skating, the next you're three bodies deep on the floor with a sudden ache you can't quite place.

But there is method to the madness—you'll find strategy, too, on the oval track.

The basics in a nutshell: Bouts usually consist of three 20-minute periods. During each period, the teams line the track for back-to-back jams, which last no more than two minutes each. Teams send out five players each for a jam (provided there's no one in the penalty box).

As for who's out there: You've got a pivot, who wears a striped cap on her helmet and leads the pack for each team. The pivots serve as the last lines of defense, but they have other duties, too, like barking instructions to the rest of the skaters and setting the pack's speed. The pack, by the way, is made up of the majority of skaters together at any given place on the track. Girls fall, they get left behind, they skate too far ahead—whatever the case—if they're more than 20 feet from the pack they're considered out of play. Unless, of course, they're the jammers.

Jammers, who wear caps with stars on them, get much of the glory (deservedly, I say), because they're the point-scoring skaters for each team. The job of these brave souls: Skate at a breakneck pace, fend off blocker hits by the baker's dozen, and get through the pack (legally) before the other jammer does to obtain lead jammer status. (Said status allows you to call off the jam anytime you'd like, a perk both teams want.) On the second pass through the pack, the jammer starts scoring points: one point for each opposing player legally passed. And what's considered legal? Jammers have to remain inbounds and get through without fouling any of the opposing team. And they do this dizzying, speed-skating, fending-off-hits thing for two minutes, or until the lead jammer calls off the jam. Sound fun? A little bit insane? Yeah, probably both.

The last three players on each team are the blockers, who serve two main purposes: Stop the opposing jammer and do whatever they can to help their jammer get through; it's your basic offense and defense stuff. And when you're on the track, it feels a lot like multitasking. Blockers are also schooled at giving "whips"—offer

an outstretched arm, the jammer grabs it and the blocker "whips" the jammer around and through. There's also a bit of containment—if you can't knock the other jammer down, get in front of her and slow her down—and there's run-of-the-mill offense where you knock the opposing blockers down, or at the very least get in their way, so they can't get to your jammer as she's passing. There's a lot to think about.

Those are just the basics. Beyond that—there are a million rules for where you can hit, what part of the body you can hit and hit with, and more. It's all a little mind-numbing. But if you get the basics of the game down, you can watch it, enjoy it, and let the refs worry their pretty little helmeted heads over the details.

Joan of Dark, a jammer for the Naptown Roller Girls, gets a little heated during a bout. Photo by Tom Klubens.

Naptown Roller Girl J. Roller takes the lead against the Hard Knox Roller Girls. Photo by Tom Klubens.

Jane Ire and Blazin' Ace of Naptown celebrate a sudden-death overtime win. Photo by Tom Klubens.

The Art

As an entity, posters have a long and storied history. With advances in color lithography and improved production techniques, poster art really took off in the 1890s—with artists and illustrators beginning to design pieces as works of art, rather than as conduits for information only. Over the decades since, posters have been increasingly used to promote pretty much everything, and the artwork itself has run the gamut, too. From the distinctive creations of Hatch Show Print, one of the oldest working letterpress print shops in America (think: vintage state fair or country music posters) to the blown-out psychedelic styles of gig posters characteristic of 1960s Haight-Ashbury, posters have been neither here nor there for too long, because they've really just been everywhere.

During the 1980s, artist Frank Kozik became a champion of the concert poster when he created visual glitter for local bands in Austin, Texas. Kozik has been credited with revitalizing poster art, though I think punk rock flier art in late-1970s New York also played a heavy hand. Other artistic movements were also falling in line around this time, and these movements, key players and artistic styles would all come to influence the posters you'll see in this book.

Famed artist Robert Williams coined the term "lowbrow" to describe the American art movement that was taking hold in the late '80s and early '90s. Williams, who'd come into his own by working for car builder Ed "Big Daddy" Roth and hooking up with many from the Zap Comix crew (Robert Crumb, Stanley Mouse, Rick Griffin, and S. Clay Wilson, among them), was gaining ground with his highly sexualized oil-rich tales about sex, violence, drugs, car culture and bodily functions. When Williams started *Juxtapoz Art & Culture* magazine in 1994, his purpose was to unearth underground and outlaw artists—like himself.

What Williams did instead: Create a world where artists, illustrators, and pop culture pundits suddenly *all* wanted to live. The new art movement shunned the conceptual- and abstract-embracing art school groupthink. It was instead inspired by B-movies, horror and science-fiction films, comic books, tattoos, hot rods, pin-up art, and pop culture. The art was narrative, it was illustrative, and it was—and kinda still is—eschewed by proponents and promoters of "high" gallery and museum art. But no matter; the greatest stuff on earth grows organically. The lowbrow movement was viral. And it spread.

Enter roller derby, another anomaly that grew its roots in the American landscape. Today's derby embraces the same ethics and values held by artists like Kozik and Williams. It feeds off grass-roots efforts, a DIY spirit, and talent, which, though it may not generally be accepted by mainstream ideals, is still both viable and laudable. Many of the artists featured in this book have grown up with—and into—a lowbrow culture. The bright colors, the bold lines, the graphic details, the illustrative approaches are all here in their work. Derby serves as the meeting ground where these influences merge with athletics—kind of an odd mix if you think about it long enough. But it's a mix that works. Clearly.

Roller derby, then, can also be considered an offshoot of an already-thriving subculture, and it continues—like lowbrow—to seep into mainstream culture. Derby gals have been featured on major news networks, on radio programs, and in television series. Even McDonald's came out with a roller derby doll to include in children's Happy Meals. And junior leagues, with high school-aged skaters, are sprouting up all over, too.

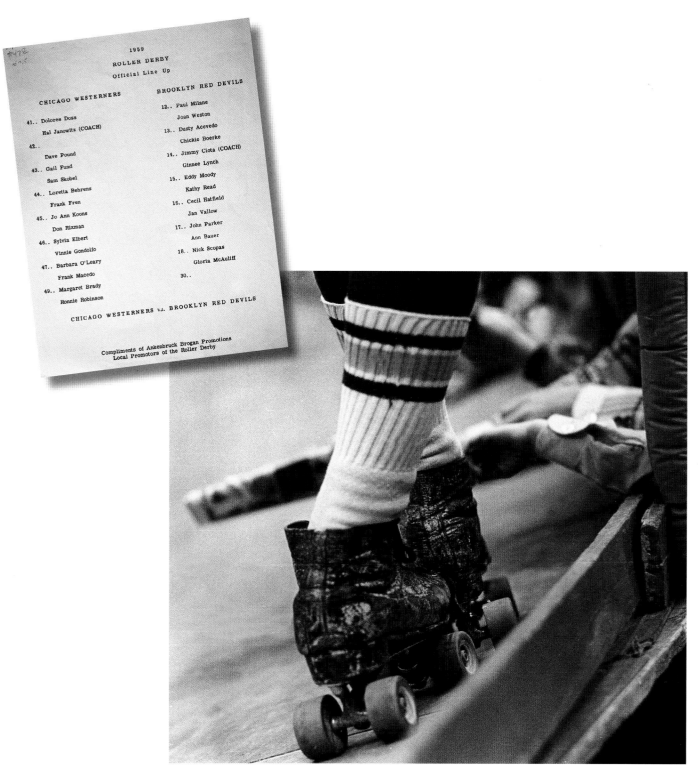

1959
ROLLER DERBY
Official Line Up

CHICAGO WESTERNERS	BROOKLYN RED DEVILS
	12.. Paul Milane
41.. Dolores Doss	Joan Weston
Hal Janowitz (COACH)	13.. Dusty Acevedo
42..	Chickie Boerke
Dave Pound	14.. Jimmy Ciota (COACH)
43.. Gail Fund	Ginnee Lynch
Sam Skobel	15.. Eddy Moody
44.. Loretta Behrens	Kathy Read
Frank Fren	16.. Cecil Hatfield
45.. Jo Ann Koons	Jan Vallow
Don Rixman	17.. John Parker
46.. Sylvia Elbert	Ann Bauer
Vinnie Gondolfo	18.. Nick Scopas
47.. Barbara O'Leary	Gloria McAuliff
Frank Macedo	30..
49.. Margaret Brady	
Ronnie Robinson	

CHICAGO WESTERNERS vs. BROOKLYN RED DEVILS

Compliments of Ankenbruck Brogan Promotions
Local Promotors of the Roller Derby

Photo by Joe Vitti.

They say, Rome wasn't built in a day. Some of the best things in life—according to little ol' me—took decades to really germinate and grow. Then there were other great achievements that we still talk about today—the beat movement, punk, a number of terrific art and film genres—that really kinda died (or at the very least dramatically morphed) before they hit their teens. So when I think back to my friend telling me roller derby is old news, it's easy to figure him for wrong—way wrong. Derby doesn't age in dog years, and the sport, as we know it, is just beginning to grow. The man in black may have sang it best, but I'm willing to heist his words for the sake of this discussion: Roller derby has been everywhere, man. I'm excited to see where next it will go.

Spinning Where? Arizona Roller Derby

An artist by trade, **Mike Maas** has a degree in graphic design and he splits his time between doing freelance illustration and pop art paintings and sculptures. His twisted humor and life-long obsession with monsters and the macabre make Maas' artwork a unique viewing experience. His influences range from the horror punk music of The Cramps to the literary experiments of the late, great Kurt Vonnegut. Throw in '60s advertising, underground comic books and classic B-movies, and you've got Maas. Find more of his work at www.greenfuzz.net.

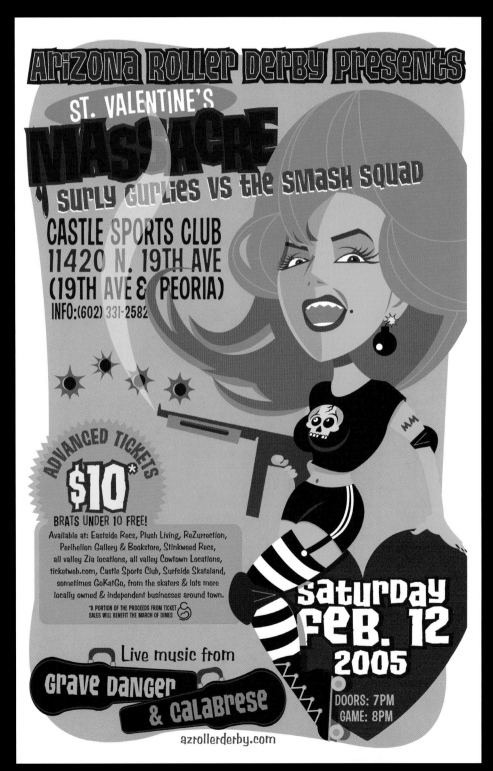

By Mike Maas

By Mike Maas

By Mike Maas

Dave Cook designs baby clothes—with cute little puppies, dinosaurs and fire trucks—by day, and monster art and roller derby posters for the Atlanta Rollergirls by night. A regular vendor at comic and horror conventions, Cook draws "Cadavitures," which are caricatures of customers as blood-oozing zombies. As a result of Cook's contribution to derby art, which he began in 2006, he is now designing gig posters, CD art, and T-shirt graphics for local and national bands. His art can be found at www.idrawmonsters.com.

Dave Cook.

Logo by Dave Cook.

23

Logo by Dave Cook.

Logo by Dave Cook.

By Dave Cook.

By Dave Cook.

By Dave Cook.

By Dave Cook.

By Dave Cook.

By Dave Cook.

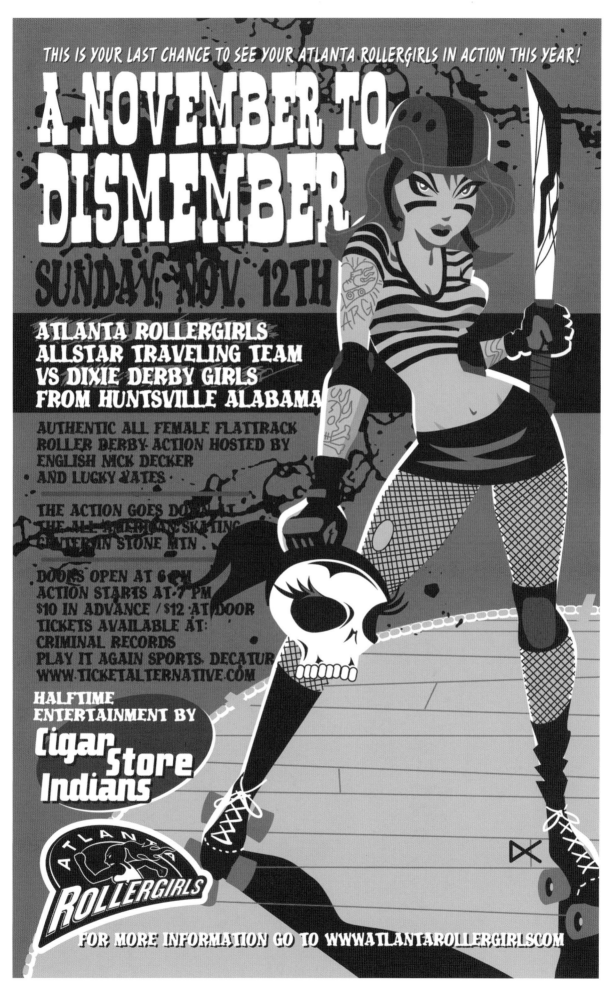

By Dave Cook.

Derek Yaniger, another artist creating posters for the Atlanta Rollergirls, has a long history of creating art for bigwigs like Marvel Comics and Cartoon Network. These days, he gets a charge out of doing art for events like the Tiki Oasis, The Rock n Roll Monster Bash and The Hukilau, as well as for magazines like Barracuda, 1313 and Tiki Magazine. Yaniger's had his paintings in galleries all over the country, including Copro/Nason in Santa Monica, Roq La Rue in Seattle and DvA Gallery in Chicago. He's also peddling his serigraphs through a heap of galleries, including Outre in Australia, M Modern in Palm Springs and online through www.misterretro. com. His scribbles can be found at www.derekart.com.

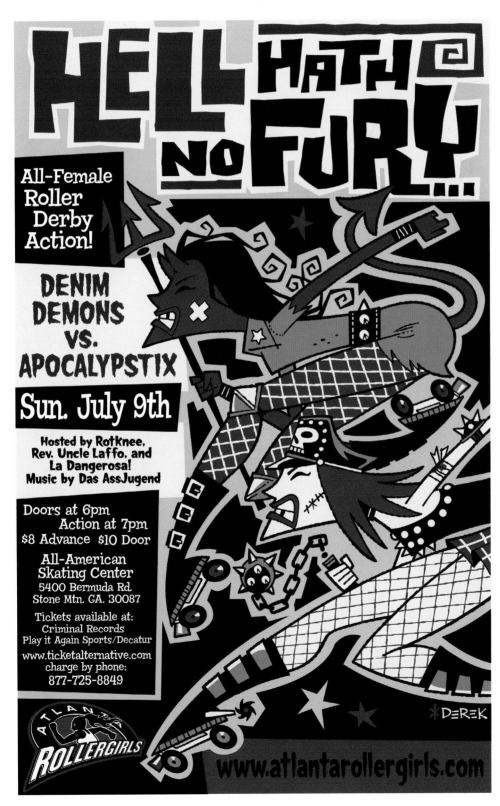

By Derek Yaniger.

The Poster Process
Artist Whiskey 7/Athena Barbital

A lot of people ask me about my process. Do I draw all of the fliers myself? Do I design them myself? How does it work? Well, I will show you. I have taken a flier for the North Star Roller Girls and dissected the process.

First, I usually get some sort of theme for a poster, then I like to turn on some music and get out a sketchbook to start sketching ideas. I always go by the six-step method. I make six sketches in six minutes, first going with the most obvious idea, a second slightly less obvious, a third that, hmm, looks pretty good, a fourth that, maybe, is getting too detailed, a fifth that gets way too complicated, and the sixth: always a picture of me getting burnt out on the idea.

I usually use the third or fourth sketch. Those tend to be the best. Not super obvious, but not too overworked.

I drew the sketches for this poster for the North Star Roller Girls on smooth Bristol paper using Alvin mechanical drafting pencils. This particular theme: "Mean, Green Fighting Machines."

So what was the obvious idea? Leprechauns for St. Paddy's Day boxing. Yeah. Boring. Been done a hundred times. Idea No. 2? A roller girl boxing a leprechaun. Idea No. 3. Man. I HATE leprechauns. They're so ugly to draw. How about just the roller girl with boxing gloves? Idea No. 4: OK. So I have a roller girl with boxing gloves. What's St. Paddy's Day about it? Why does that fit in with a "Mean, Green Fighting Machine" theme anyway? So I put a big green dress on her and make her look beat up, or, how about making her into a beauty queen? Those ladies would do anything to win.

After going through a few more ideas and getting way too complicated with the idea (hand drawing clovers on her entire dress), I settled on idea No. 4—a beat-up beauty queen in boxing gloves wearing a giant, fluffy, green dress. Mean Green Fighting Machine. That works.

So I busted out my tools of the trade, and did a rough sketch of my idea. This is what it looked like:

Next, I send the sketch to the chair of North Star Roller Girls marketing committee to get the idea approved before I spend too much time and energy on it. Once she gives the thumbs up or down, I then start to ink it in. I usually use a vast array of technical pens usually starting with a .03 Alvin to make the first initial sweep, and then working on my line quality by going over certain areas with a .05, and then a .08 to try to create the sense of overlapping and depth.

After that I take my favorite pen in the world, a Sakura Pigma brush pen in pure black, and outline the whole drawing in it. I love this pen because it has a brush for a tip that lays the ink down for you. It's a very organic feel, and it takes some getting used to. Once the inking is done, I erase away all the pencil lines, and then scan it into the computer. The drawing then usually ends up looking like this:

Once I get the image scanned, I can then start plugging in the different colors to find a palette I like. From this point on, it's a lot like coloring in a coloring book, and it's my favorite part of the process. Once the basic colors are laid in, I can start working on details like the highlights and the shadows.

Once I get that done, I can start adding fonts:

Usually there are a few more changes, and once we get all the fine-tuning done, we have a finished derby poster.

Becoming a Derby Girl
—and a derby poster art girl

Whiskey7/Athena Barbital #95mg
Pivot/Blocker/Captain
Sin City Roller Girls
www.myspace.com/double_whiskey7

You can say this whole addiction started for me in the late summer of 2004. I was at one of my favorite local haunts when the bartender handed me a postcard with Rosie the Riveter on it. The postcard said, "We Can Do It."

"Damn girl. You would have an awesome body for this!"

The funny thing was, I was a bit offended by that, rolled my eyes, and put the postcard in my purse without looking at it. About a week later I was cleaning out my bag when I came across it again. Roller derby. Weird.

I skateboarded when I was younger and I was quite the little daredevil. However, for the last six years I had been playing in bands, touring around the country and drinking a lot. I had a beer belly to prove it. Still, I decided to go to the first recruitment party.

The rest, you can say, is history.

I had started doing poster art way back when I began playing in bands in 1996. Usually I would draw everything out by hand—including all the fonts—with a Sharpie, and then go to the local Kinkos to make black-and-white photocopies. I was a real high-tech kinda gal.

When I graduated from high school, I decided to pursue a career in art. I graduated from the Minneapolis College of Art and Design (MCAD) with a short stint at Parsons School of Design in Paris, France.

When I joined up with the Minnesota RollerGirls in 2004, years after I graduated from college, I realized the need for posters. There had to be posters for everything! I unleashed my squeaky design skills unto the world and, with much help from my designer friends, started making derby posters.

I ended up taking a break from derby for a while after my first derby season to focus on my band. It wasn't long before I got the "Derby DTs" and couldn't stay away. In 2005, I ended up joining another local Minneapolis league called the TC Rollers. It was a bit different. It was a privately owned, non-democratic league.

I finished out the season there as captain of the Kilmore Girls. My future derby wife, Roller Vixen, captain of our rival team, The Banger Sisters, and I spent a lot of time commiserating in her garage over whiskey 7s in the wee hours of the morning. There were times when a whole weekend would go by and we'd realize that I hadn't gone home yet. We figure all the good and bad things in our lives happened over a few too many whiskeys in the garage; hence the name I decided to use for my art.

Vixen and I eventually decided that we should see if there was interest in starting up a skater-owned league with the 60-plus skaters involved with the TC Rollers. Before we knew it, about 99 percent of the skaters sent in letters of resignation to the owner of the TC Rollers. The North Star Roller Girls were born.

The North Star Roller Girls were 100-percent skater-owned and -operated, and the league was democratically run. It's still skating strong with 80 skaters and a support staff that could make your head spin.

Soon after the North Star Roller Girls were formed, a large group of us attended our first RollerCon in Las Vegas. Meeting skaters from all over the world was too much for me to handle. I decided I wanted to make poster art for everyone and their mama, so I made some fliers to start doing free posters for any league that would have me.

Sin City Roller Girls took me up on my offer. And the list goes on. I am proud to say I've made posters for leagues such as Angel City, Duke City Derby, Rocky Mountain, Mad Rollin' Dolls, Minnesota RollerGirls, Pikes Peak, Arizona Roller Derby, Dominion, Ottawa, Oil City, Vancouver, and Conneticut.

I served as the art director for the 2007 RollerCon, and I donated prints of my entire portfolio to raise money for women's health education through Planned Parenthood. This donation was in honor of Traylor Crash, Dominion's founder who had recently passed away from terminal cancer. I also was offered a place to stay and a spot as a skater on the Sin City Roller Girls, should I ever decide to move to Las Vegas.

At the end of my 2007 season, I decided to take a chance and move to Vegas to skate as a Sin City Roller Girl. Entering my fourth season as a derby girl, I wasn't sure how much steam I had left, and I definitely wanted to experience traveling and playing in inter-league bouts before my body had reached its maximum pain threshold. (At this point, I had fractured a kneecap, sprained my right knee, torn ligaments on both knees, sprained my shoulder, suffered multiple butt and shoulder contusions, gotten stress fractures in my right ankle, chronic tendonitis in both knees, and muscle spasms in my lower back).

In the meantime, I started doing more artwork for leagues. I usually only book one to two posters a month, and I quickly found myself booked months ahead of schedule. I was offered a season contract with Duke City Derby, which was the first league to offer to compensate me for my services. Soon after, I signed another contract with Oil City Derby Girls. Leagues started offering me compensation for my time through trades, plane tickets, or just cash in order to get their posters on time.

After talking to a few of the girls on Duke City about what they were looking for in terms of art for their 2007 season, we decided it would be cool to feature each of their home teams. I did the team poster for the Hobots, the Doomsdames, and the Derby Intelligence Agency. Those were some of my favorite posters to make. I loved how creative the individual teams were with their identities.

The last four years have been amazing so far. The more I make roller derby art and skate, the more addicted I am to it. Las Vegas really is a city based off of luck, and so far I feel I've been pretty lucky. I found a job working as a professional graphic designer within 24 hours of getting off the plane, and I'm always impressed by the talent, honesty and sincerity of the girls I am honored to call my team. I'm very proud to have recently been voted in as a captain of the Sin City Roller Girls!

By Athena Barbital.

LIVE ROLLER DERBY!
CT ROLLER GIRLS PRESENT
Spring Break!
SUNDAY APRIL FIRST 2007

DOORS
5:30
BOUT
6:30

$12/ADV.
$15/DOOR
$25
VIP TICKETS

WIDOWMAKERS VS. IRON ANGELS
FEATURING DJ E-BOMB!
KIDS UNDER 12 FREE WITH PAYING ADULT
Roller Magic 60 Harvester Road (off S. Main st) Waterbury

Poster by
Whiskey 7

for tickets and more info

WWW.CTROLLERDERBY.COM
www.myspace.com/double_whiskey7

By Athena Barbital.

By Athena Barbital.

By Athena Barbital.

By Athena Barbital.

By Athena Barbital.

Dairyland Dolls

Mad Rollin Dolls Present Live Roller Derby

MAD ROLLIN' DOLLS   ROCKY MOUNTAIN ROLLERGIRLS

Rollergirls

DAIRYLAND DOLLS

From Madison, Wisconsin

DOORS 6:30
BOUT 7:30

Half Time
**FEATURING
YWCA GIRL
NEIGHBORHOOD
POWER**
*Double Dutch and a
Drill Team*

CHARITY *Outreach*
WWW.OUTREACHINC.COM

5280 FIGHT CLUB

From Denver, Colorado

OCT. 20TH
$10/ADV.
$12/DOOR

AFTER PARTY
100 BLOCK OF WEST MAIN
*Specials at the Paradise
and The Shamrock*

TICKET OUTLETS
FAST FORWARD, FREEDOM/KNUCKLEHEADS
CAPITAL CITY TATTOO, CHACHA BARBER
AND BEAUTY PARLOR, HIGH NOON
SALOON, AND LAKESIDE PRESS.

FAST FORWARD
SKATE CENTER
4649 Verona Road

DERBY HOTLINE
608.271.6222
EXT.150

MAD ROLLIN' DOLLS
HURT IN A SKIRT

WWW.MADROLLINDOLLS.COM

MAD ROLLIN' DOLLS
HURT IN A SKIRT

Poster By Whiskey 7 ★★★ www.myspace.com/double_whiskey7

By Athena Barbital.

46

By Athena Barbital.

The North Star Roller Girls are Proud to Host

MARK MALLMANS NEW YEARS EVE

Bash!

Mark Mallman

Vicious Vicious

Solid Gold

$10 adv.
$12 at the door
8PM DEC. 31ST

d.j. Jake Rudh

VARSITY THEATER
1308 4th St. SE, Minneapolis, MN

presented by: vita.mn 89.3 the current

www.northstarrollergirls.com
www.mallman.com
www.varsitytheater.org to get your tickets now!

N.S.R.G.

By Athena Barbital.

By Athena Barbital.

By Athena Barbital.

By Athena Barbital.

By Athena Barbital.

By Athena Barbital.

By Athena Barbital.

By Athena Barbital.

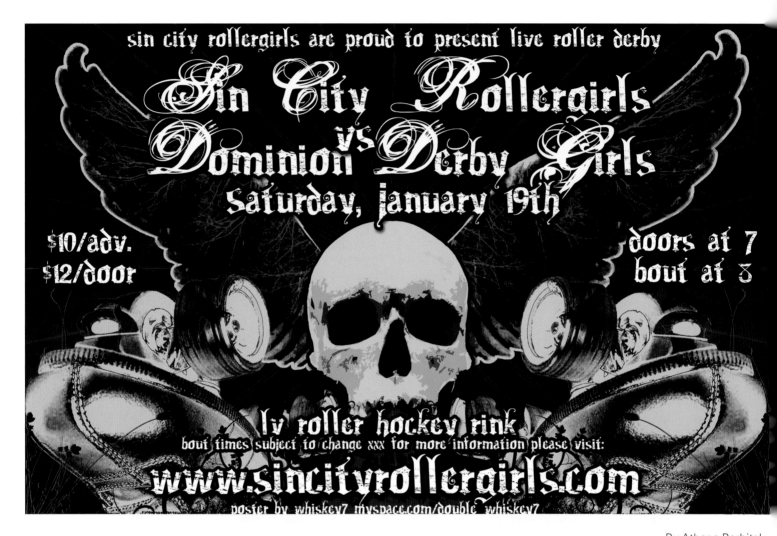

sin city rollergirls are proud to present live roller derby

Sin City Rollergirls
vs Dominion Derby Girls
Saturday, January 19th

$10/adv.
$12/door

doors at 7
bout at 8

lv roller hockey rink
bout times subject to change xxx for more information please visit:

www.sincityrollergirls.com
poster by whiskey7 myspace.com/double_whiskey7

By Athena Barbital.

Black -N- Bluegrass Girls

Angela Kilduff, who skates under the name Florence Maul, designed and produced the Black -N- Bluegrass posters with Clay Brunton from PowerHouse Factories in Ohio. Though she was a member of the Black -N- Bluegrass Rollergirls when she created these posters, Kilduff now skates with the Cincinnati Rollergirls.

"I started hearing more and more about roller derby and got involved after talking to a roller girl one night at a bar. I was drawn to the speed, strength, and unapologetic attitude of the sport. … My roller derby friends are strong saucy women whose company I love. We skate, gossip, laugh, go out, and travel together. We come from different backgrounds and different lives, but derby unites us all."
Angela Kilduff, aka Florence Maul

By Angela Kilduff and Clay Brunton of PowerHouse Factories.

By Angela Kilduff and Clay Brunton of PowerHouse Factories for the Riverside Rollergirls.

Boston Derby Dames

Colleen Simon, aka Rocky, is an interior designer, a Boston Derby Dame, and a closet graphic designer. With a bachelor of fine arts degree in interior design from Syracuse University, Simon works for a commercial architecture, interior and graphic design firm. She is a blocker and—occasionally—a jammer.

"I found the Boston Derby Dames in January 2006 while looking for a new sport to play and a way to relieve stress, and, after attending one practice, I knew roller derby was my kind of sport, team-oriented, full-contact, and full of awesome women. I think the roller derby resurgence is an amazing and positive movement for women. It is great to see women thrive within a sport we have literally made our own. I have always been an athletic person and a huge professional sports fan, but to be a part of a sport, organization and a movement that has been uniquely successful to women alone is incredibly rewarding."

Colleen Simon, aka Rocky

Colleen Simon, also known as the Boston Derby Dame "Rocky."

BOSTON MASSACRE vs. PHILADELPHIA LIBERTY BELLES

SLAUGHTERS OF THE REVOLUTION

LIVE ROLLER DERBY

SATURDAY FEBRUARY 10TH

SHRINERS AUDITORIUM WILMINGTON, MA

DOORS AT 5PM
BOUT AT 6PM
$14 ONLINE
$16 AT DOOR
CHILDREN UNDER 6 FREE

AFTER PARTY AT SHRINERS

LIVE PERFORMANCES BY THE DENTS & DJ BOO BOO DANGER

FREE PARKING OR SHUTTLE FROM COMMUTER RAIL

FOR TICKETS AND INFORMATION VISIT
WWW.BOSTONDERBYDAMES.COM

Boston Derby Dames are proud members of the Women's Flat Track Derby Association

Photography by Scott Engelhardt, Artwork by Colleen Simon

By Colleen Simon.

PROM NIGHT
DRESS TO KILL!

starring BOSTON DERBY DAMES

FEATURING
DJ BOO BOO DANGER
ALL FIRED UP - 80'S COVER BAND

THURSDAY APRIL 20TH
BILL'S BAR - LANSDOWNE ST - $8 FOR 21+, $10 FOR 18+
PROM QUEEN, KING AND PRIZES FOR BEST & WORST DRESSED

By Colleen Simon.

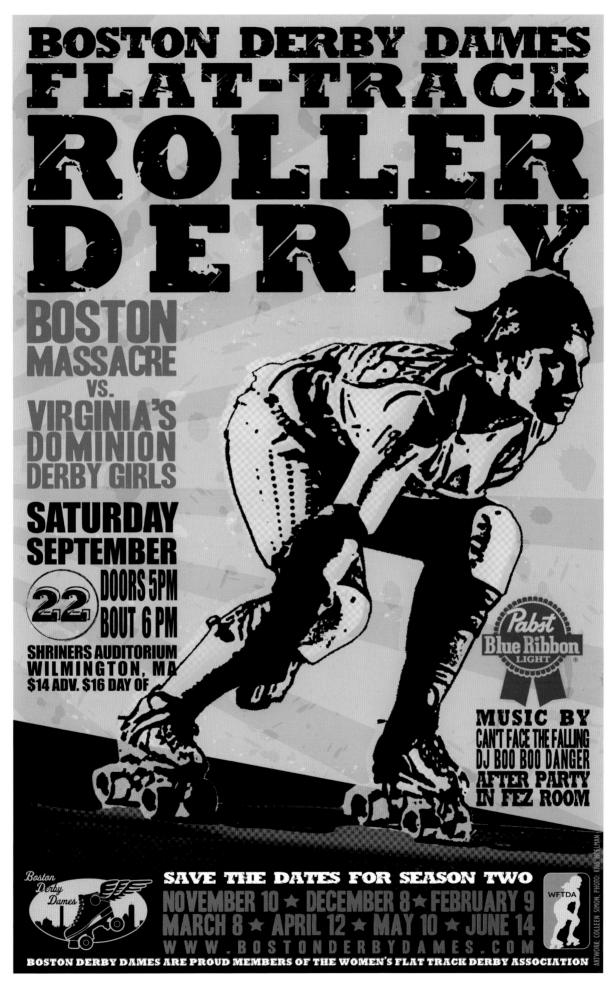

By Colleen Simon.

By Colleen Simon.

By Colleen Simon.

has suffered two minor concussions and a torn PCL in her knee, but she says she's "pretty good on crutches now." More of her work can be found at www.livwrongdesign.com.

By Liv Wrong Design.

Adam Potts is a full-time tattoo artist by trade, but from time to time he donates his time and talent to the ladies of the Derby City Roller Girls. The reason he's not a roller girl, he says, is due mostly to gender bias—not because of his complete lack of skating skill. Where his lack of talent on wheels leaves off, however, his artistic skill begins.

Find more of his art at www.myspace.com/adamacmeink.

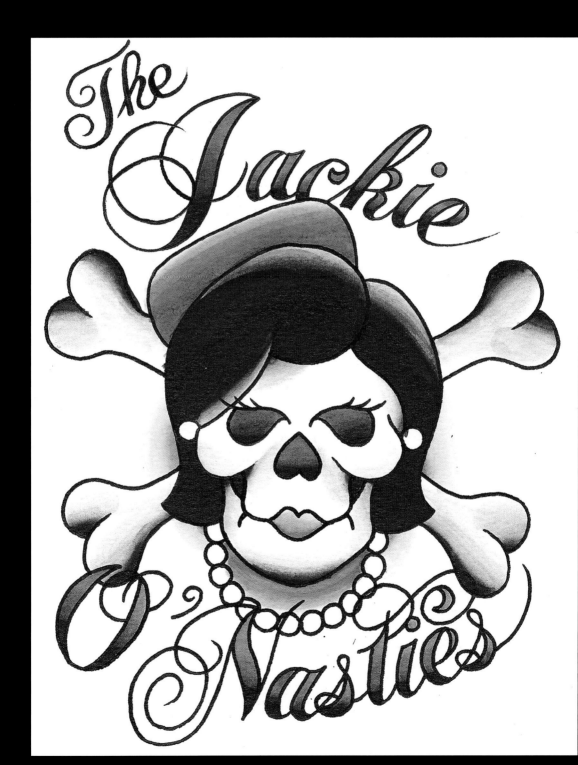

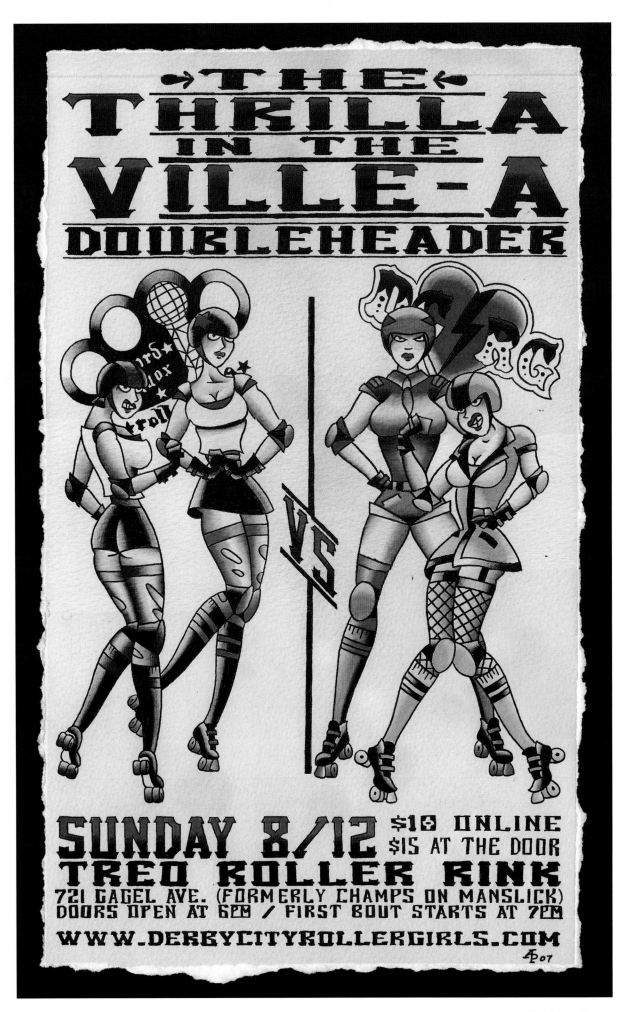

By Adam Potts.

E-Ville Roller Derby

Veronica Scallion, also known as Hexx Luther, proudly claims her roller girl status as a blocker with the E-Ville Roller Derby league. A graphic designer by trade, Scallion, who found roller derby in 2007, posts her more personal work on www.veronicascallion.com.

By Veronica Scallion (Hexx Luther).

Rev. Chad Wells is a heavily published writer and multi-award-winning tattoo artist. Wells also has created posters, shirts and album covers for dozens of well-known bands, ranging from Electric Frankenstein to Deicide, and for roller derby teams like the Gem City Rollergirls and Mississippi Rollergirls. Wells also served as the frontman for the incendiary punk band The Jackalopes, and he is half of the creative team behind AartKult Clothing and Art Publishing Company. More of his work can be found at www.wellstattoo.com.

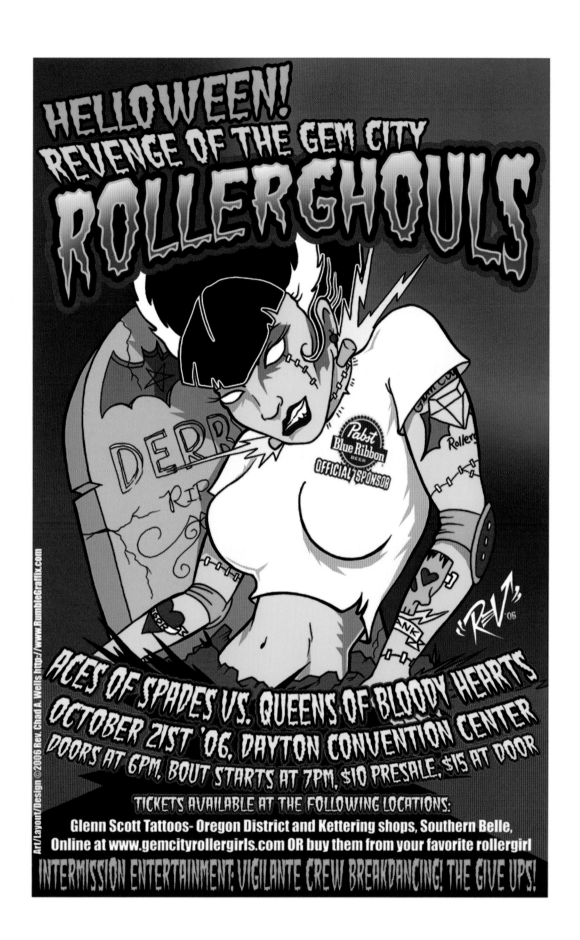

By Rev. Chad Wells.

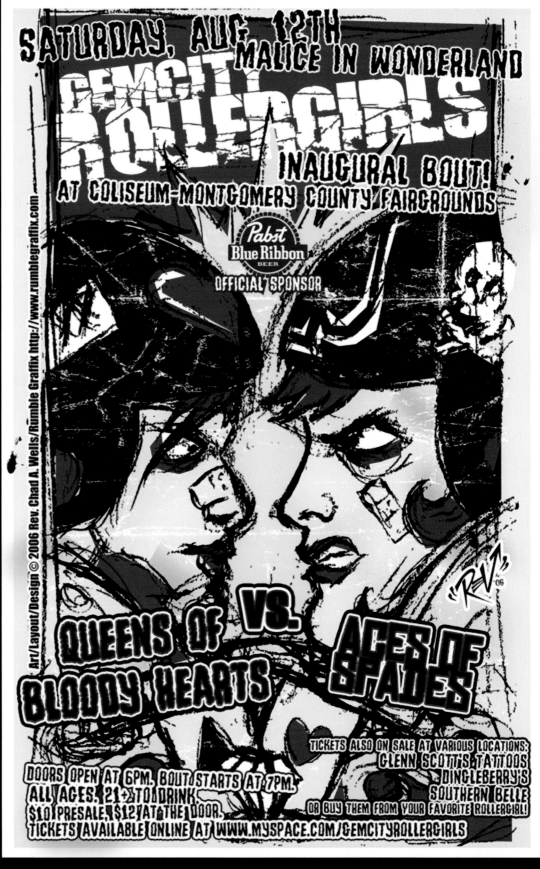

Logo by Rev. Chad Wells.

SATURDAY, JULY 27TH
FULL CONTACT!
MUSICAL CHAIRS
FEATURING THE
GEM CITY ROLLERGIRLS
AT DAYTON GYM CLUB
430 WAYNE AVE, DAYTON, OH

WHO WILL BE
of the
Queen Chairs
?

THE BANG TALE · THE JACKALOPES
HOT CARL & THE RUSTY TROMBONES
WWW.GEMCITYROLLERGIRLS.COM

18+up/21 to Drink, Doors 7pm, Chairs start at 8pm, $5 cover
Art/Layout/Design ©2006 Rev. Wells www.rumblegraffix.com

By Rev. Chad Wells

By Rev. Chad Wells.

With an education at the School of Visual Arts in New York for illustration, **Cully Long** now serves as a scenic and costume designer for theatre in New York City. Long has always been influenced by comic book art, and his recent works include sketches done while riding NYC's subways. That work can be found at childofatom.blogspot.com/search/label/subway. For Long's other art, head to www.cullylong.com.

Cully Long.

By Cully Long.

Wendi Koontz was once a tattoo artist, but these days she's working as an illustrator in New York City. Koontz, who claims she's really "not a big sports person," was drawn to derby because of the excitement of the sport. Her art can be found at www.wendikoontz.com.

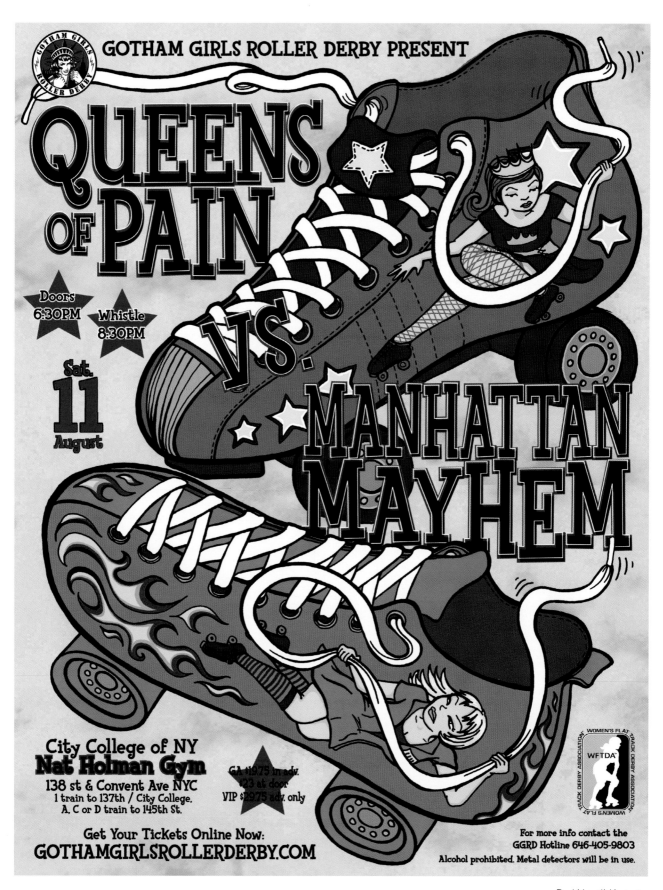

By Wendi Koontz.

Taking his influences from comic books, surrealism, politics, pop culture, photorealism and cartoons, **Rob Israel** works in illustration and design. His art can be found at www.robworld.org.

Rob Israel.

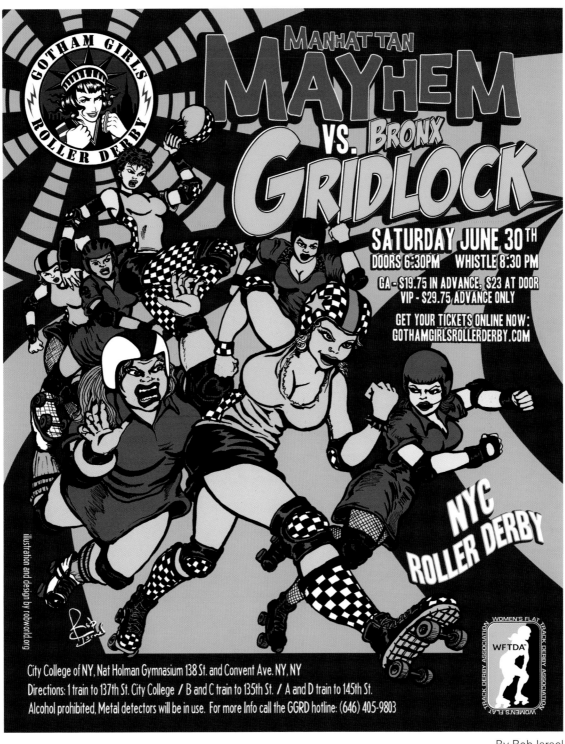

By Rob Israel.

By Rob Israel

Based in New York City, **Joe Simko** designs illustrations for local and national rock bands; he was the official artist for the 2006 Vans Warped Tour, and Japan's 2007 MAGMA Rock Festival. Simko has created art for all kinds of clients, including skateboard and snowboard companies, custom guitar manufacturers and publishers of graphic novels. Simko's style gravitates toward the Saturday morning cartoon art of the 1980s. Influenced by cereal box art and MAD magazine, Simko says his art was corrupted by his equal love for dark comics and movies. He likes to use bright colorful imagery with grim situations and often with hidden subliminal undertones. His work can be found at www.sweetrot.com.

Joe Simko.

By Joe Simko.

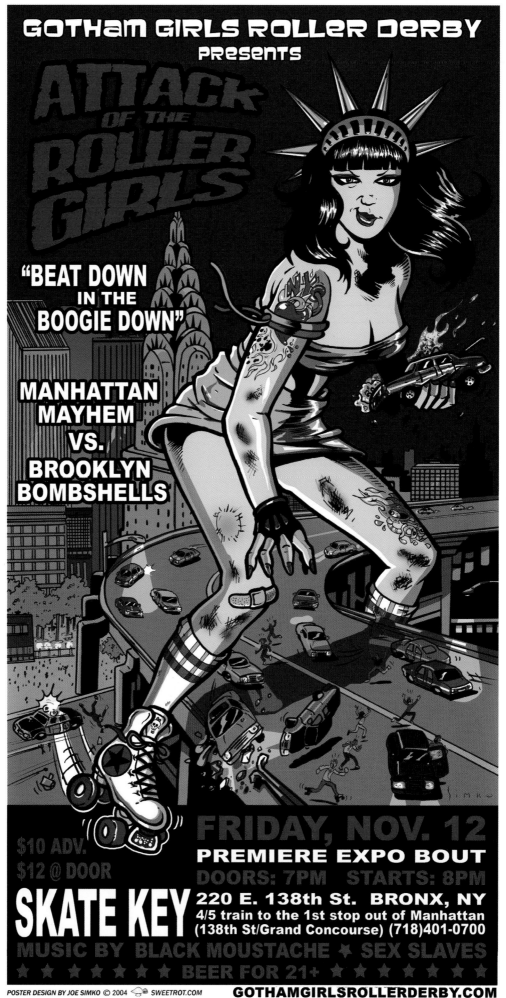

By Joe Simko.

Nicole Walker, graphic designer and illustrator from Hamilton, Ontario, has been a member of the Hammer City Roller Girls since May of 2007. Beyond her day job and the freelance illustration and design work she brings in, Walker has tried her hand at making jewelry, silversmithing, knitting, painting, airbrushing, and more. You can find her work at www.glacier-grrl.deviantart.com.

By Nicole Walker

L.A. Derby Dolls

Sandra Frame (Tara Armov) skates with the L.A. Derby Dolls, a banked-track league in Los Angeles, California that she joined in January of 2004. Frame is a storyboard artist with credits on several shows, including *The Simpsons*, *Pinky and the Brain*, and *Scooby Doo*. She says her style is definitely "cartoony and whimsical," and I take a lot of inspiration from Maurice Sendak, Shel Silverstein, Dr. Seuss, and old Warner Bros cartoons.

Armov first heard of roller derby when she was living in Dallas, Texas and a friend suggested she check out the Texas Rollergirls in Austin. Instead, Armov found her way to a Lonestar Rollergirls (the city's banked-track league) event, and from there, she tells her story:

> I didn't know what to expect, but what I saw was a huge warehouse with spray-painted banners on the walls, old theater seats strewn all over the floor, which surrounded a banked track. Then I noticed the girls … tough-looking, but approachable. Punk rock, but without the snotty attitude. They were beautiful, but not in any usual Barbie doll way. I felt like I was among friends even though I didn't know any of them. This was obviously a DIY operation, and that really impressed me, since so much globalization in the marketplace is now the norm. To find something homegrown these days is a rare treat. I thought to myself, "If I were 10 years younger, I'd be so into this!" Never mind that I'd never been into sports of any sort throughout my life.

> I took that memory back to L.A. when my job ended a month later, and then I found an ad on Craig's List from the newly formed L.A. Derby Dolls, looking for skaters. I e-mailed them back saying that if they're doing what those Texas girls were doing, I'd come see their games when they started having them. League founder Thora Zeen e-mailed me back saying I should come to a practice. I said I was too old. She replied with, 'The hell you are! Get down here!' I figured, 'What do I have to lose, except maybe the use of my legs?' and so I went to a rink in the San Fernando Valley with the expectation that I'd fall a lot, get hurt, not skate anymore and carry on with my normal life. Instead, my life got turned upside-down for the better when I met and skated with the Derby Dolls.

Since my humble start with the Derby Dolls, I've become heavily involved with the league and roller derby as a whole. I was team captain of the Fight Crew for two-and-a-half years, and in our first full season my team was undefeated and won the season championship. I'm also part of the league's training team, and was heavily involved with the league's art department for a couple of years. I'm also online a lot on various roller girl forums and go to RollerCon every year. I've now started to go around to other California leagues to help train them.

I'm primarily a blocker. My injuries compared to some other skaters have been minor: twisted ligaments in my knees, sore ankles, strained shoulders and of course bruises galore. My most serious injury to date was a concussion that I received when I went flying off the high side of the track during a practice in August 2006. The highest point of the track is just over four feet, and then when you add my height of 5'10" on top of that, well, that's a good length to be falling from. I landed on my back and cracked my head on the pavement. Those helmets we're forced to wear really are good for something! I couldn't skate for a few weeks afterward due to dizzy spells, but have gotten back into the fray since then. Though I still get dizzy spells if I'm really dehydrated.

I think the popularity of the all-girl leagues is due to several factors. This is one of the few contact sports that women can play. One doesn't have to have a tiny little fashion model body to play. It's still a meritocracy … you get out what you put in. There's an incredible amount of women who aren't buying into the Bratz/Paris Hilton/Crack-pack expectations that one constantly sees in the media and advertising, and we didn't find each other until roller derby. The self-confidence boost is incredible, as is the exercise and fit muscles. We now have something to talk about that isn't vapid and pointless. We draw fans in with unorthodox outfits and names, and we keep them by showing them that just because we're not sponsored by Nike doesn't make us any less of an athlete who uses her strength and strategy to win the game. It's awesome.

Sandra Frame (Tara Armov) of the L.A. Derby Dolls.

Logo by Sandra Frame.

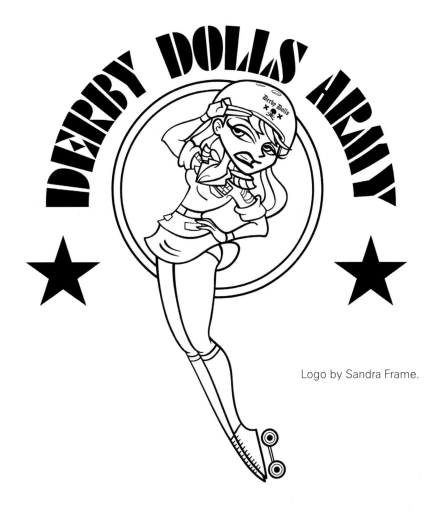

Logo by Sandra Frame.

L.A. DERBY DOLLS

Logo by Sandra Frame.

Logo by Sandra Frame.

Angel City Derby Girls

presents

ALL HELL BREAKS LOOSE!

⚡exhibition bout⚡

$10

all ages
___
21+ bar
w/ID

Friday, June 30
doors at 10:30pm
angels reign at midnite

World on Wheels
4645 1/2 Venice Blvd.
LA, CA 90019
downstairs from the bowling alley

featuring
Thee Cannibals
DJ Anita Kill

special appearance by
Techno Destructo
of **GWAR**

⚡ Holy Communion pre-funk party ⚡
9-10:30pm in the WOW bar ⚡

⚡ Costumes HIGHLY encouraged ⚡
⚡ strap on your wheels and skate with the Angels...if you dare ⚡
⚡ www.angelcityderbygirls.com ⚡
⚡ www.myspace.com/angelcityderbygirls ⚡

Angel City poster by Sandra Frame.

TAHA ARMOV 05

LA DERBY DOLLS

EXHIBITION BOUT   SIRENS V. TOUGH COOKIES

SATURDAY, JANUARY 29 8PM

1460 NAUD ST. CHINATOWN $10

SKIRTS, SKATES, SCARS

LA DERBY DOLLS
PRESENTS

BIG TROUBLE
IN LITTLE CHINATOWN

FEATURING:

SIRENS
VS.
FIGHT
CREW

SAT. MAR. 12 8PM
1460 NAUD ST.
CHINATOWN 21+

SKIRTS, SKATES, SCARS

TARA ARMOV '05

By Sandra Frame.

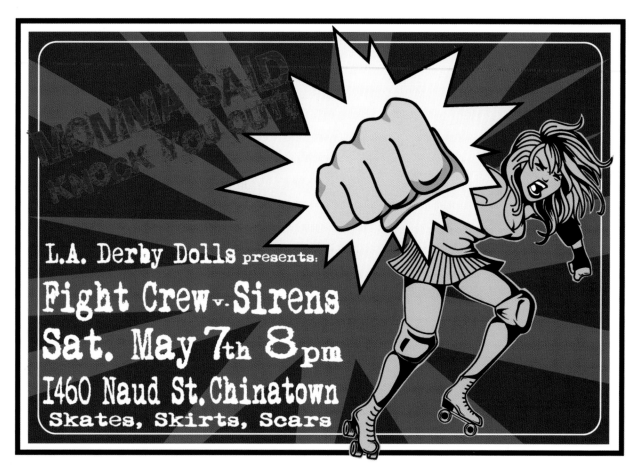

By Sandra Frame.

By Sandra Frame.

By Sandra Frame.

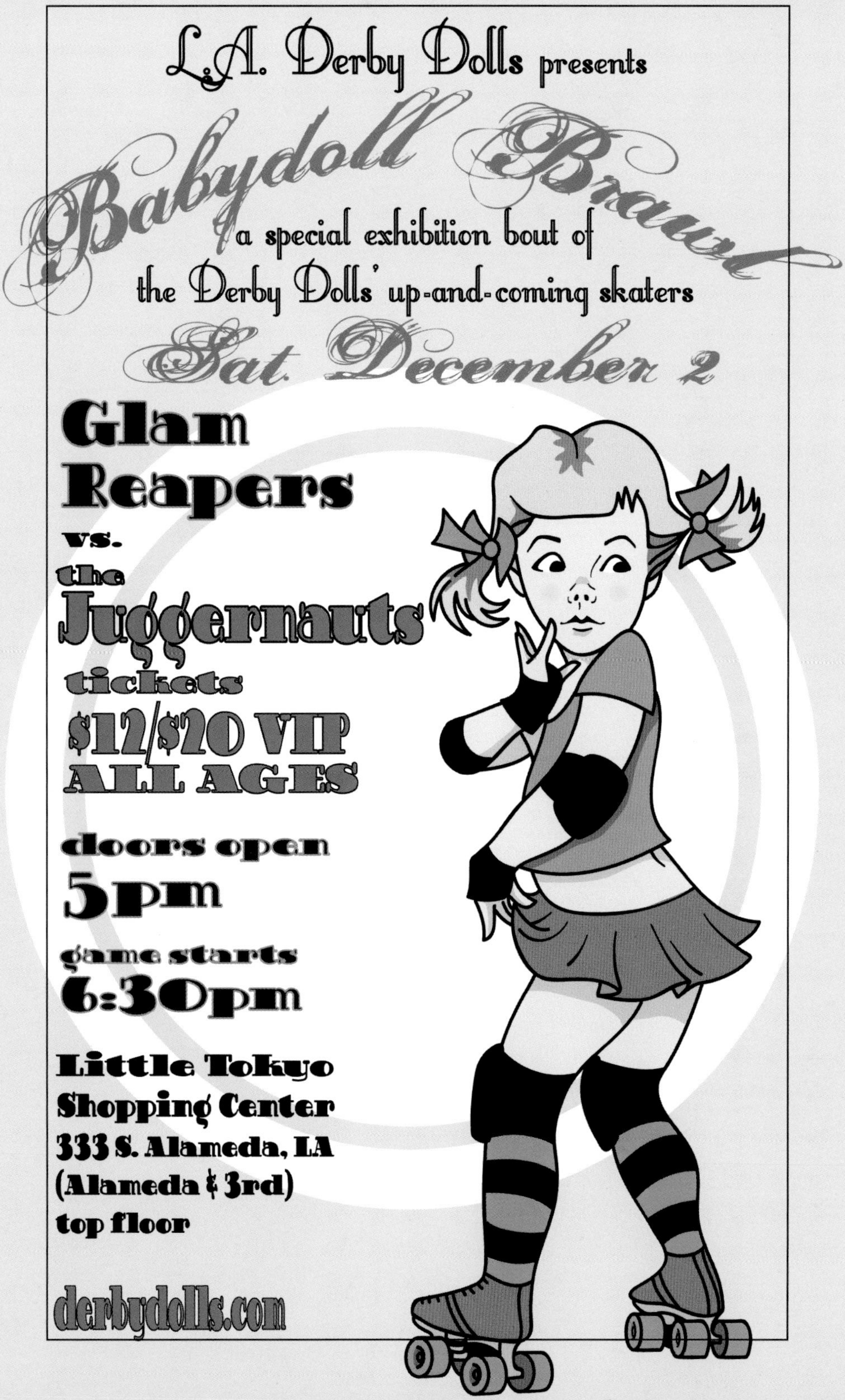
L.A. Derby Dolls presents
Babydoll Brawl
a special exhibition bout of
the Derby Dolls' up-and-coming skaters
Sat. December 2
Glam Reapers
vs.
the Juggernauts
tickets
$12/$20 VIP
ALL AGES
doors open
5pm
game starts
6:30pm
Little Tokyo
Shopping Center
333 S. Alameda, LA
(Alameda & 3rd)
top floor
derbydolls.com

By Sandra Frame

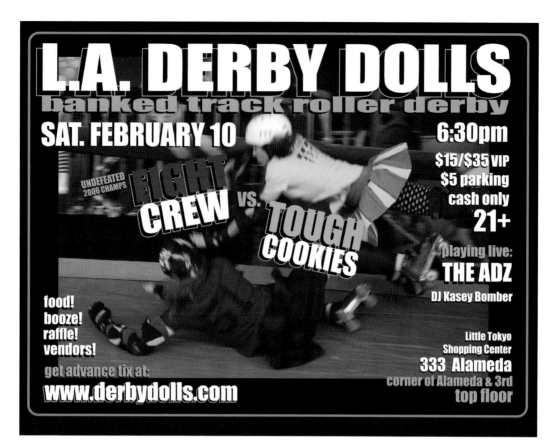

By Sandra Frame.

By Sandra Frame.

Lindsay Parker is also known as The Killustrator on the track. When she's not skating, she's designing poster art for the Lehigh Valley Roller Girls, which was established in 2006. Parker, a full-time medical illustrator, also co-owns an independent craft shop called Without A Pulse. Parker's Web sites are www.lparker.org and www.withoutapulse.com.

"Compared to our skaters who've had broken bones and displaced hips, any injuries I've sustained aren't worth mentioning. (Unless you count racking myself with my skate wheel, which was pretty gruesome.)"
Lindsay Parker

Lindsay Parker

By Lindsay Parker.

SYMBOL OF SORROW
SEDUCE THE MACHINE
AGONY OF SOUL
PEARL HEART
BACK TO BACK

@ CLUB MIXX (FORMERLY TK'S LOUNGE) ONLY $10!
****** TO BENEFIT THE ******
LEHIGH VALLEY ROLLER GIRLS
6/23/07 DOORS 8, BANDS 8:30
WWW.LVROLLERGIRLS.NET
WWW.MYSPACE.COM/LEHIGHVALLEYROLLERGIRLS

By Lindsay Parker.

94

SCHOOL'S OUT SHOWDOWN

LEHIGH VALLEY HISSYFITS

VERSUS THE MORRISTOWN MADAMS

@ ROLLERMOTION
1609 TREXLERTOWN RD
MACUNGIE, PA 18062

VISIT
WWW.MYSPACE.COM/
LEHIGHVALLEYROLLERGIRLS
or WWW.LVROLLERGIRLS.NET
FOR MORE INFORMATION

DOORS @ 5 PM JUNE 10, 2007 BOUT @ 6 PM

By Lindsay Parker.

Long Island Roller Rebels

Jessica Herber, also known as Trigger Happy Jackie, was drawn to joining the Long Island Roller Rebels because it "gives women the chance to express themselves creatively and athletically at the same time," she said. "There are very few arenas that allow these two forces to come together." Herber maintains the Web site for LIRR, and she serves as a blocker and pivot when she's on the track. More of her work can be found at www.myspace.com/sickasin.

Michael Herber, Trigger Happy Jackie's husband, is a graphic artist and Web designer who creates "dark designs," tattoo and hot rod-inspired works. His art can be found at www.myspace.com/trixxx_deezigns.

Jorge Cabrera is an artist by trade who dabbles in comic book-style work. More about the artist can be found at www.myspace.com/bizarro1213.

Jessica Herber, also known as Trigger Happy Jackie.

Michael Herber.

Jorge Cabrera.

A Night Out with Long Islands Only
All FEMALE ROLLER DERBY LEAGUE

SATURDAY, FEBRUARY 17TH AT 8PM
$5 AT THE DOOR
21+ WITH VALID ID

Arm Wrestle a Roller Girl

Shot Girls on Skates

Raffles

Beer Pong & Much Much More

Beenzy's
Bar and Grill
2955 Merrick Rd
Wantagh, NY 11710
www.Beenzysbar.com

LI
ROLLER REBELS

Now Recruiting - Skaters, Refs & Volunteers
Visit www.LongIslandRollerRebels.com

By Jessica Herber.

the Long Island Roller Rebels present...

The Ladies of Laceration
vs The Rolling Thundercats

May 12, 2007 Doors: 7pm Whistle: 8pm
Skate Safe America |182 Bethpage Sweet Hollow Rd
Old Bethpage, NY 11804 | 516.249.1717

Blackwood
myspace.com/blackwoodtheband
live dj, raffles, door prizes and more

BEVERAGE
tent will
open @
6pm

PURCHASE TICKETS NOW

TICKETS:
$12 advance
$15 door
PURCHASE TICKETS @
Skate Safe
Looney Tunes Record Store
or through
www.brownpapertickets.com
keyword: Long Island Roller Rebels

ROLLER REBELS

Don't Forget to Bring Your Chair
FUN FOR THE WHOLE FAMILY!

Drawings by Jorge Cabrera, design by Michael Herber, layout by Jessica Herber.

the Long Island Roller Rebels present...

ROLLER DERBY ACTION!!!

Wicked Wheelers vs Ladies of Laceration

July 14th 2007 Doors: 7pm Whistle: 8pm

Skate Safe America : 182 Bethpage Sweet Hollow Road
Old Bethpage, NY 11804 : 516.249.1717

Music Entertainment by
DJ Andre Bermudez
and LIVE Music by
The Anabolics

RAFFLES & PRIZES

Don't Forget to Bring Your Chair!

Beverage Tent at 6 pm

Tickets $12 adv $15 door

Buy tix at Skate Safe, Looney Tunes, Funtazia, Utopia (Centereach location) or www.LongIslandRollerRebels.com

ROLLER REBELS

www.LongIslandRollerRebels.com

Drawings by Jorge Cabrera, design by Michael Herber, layout by Jessica Herber.

THE LONG ISLAND ROLLER REBELS PRESENT...
2007 Roller Derby Championship
The Mid-Island Rolling Thundercats
vs.
The Wicked Wheelers of the West

September 15, 2007

The New York
Shock
Exchange
at 6:30 PM

Skate Safe America
182 Bethpage Sweet Hollow Road
Old Bethpage, NY 11804
516.249.1717

Don't Forget To Bring
Your Own Chairs

Buy A Booster
To Support
Your Rollergirl!

Doors @ 5:30
LIRR Whistle @ 8 p.m.
Beverage Tent @ 6pm

Buy tix at
Skate Safe,
Looney Tunes, Funtazia,
Utopia (Centereach location) or
www.LongIslandRollerRebels.com

WWW.LONGISLANDROLLERREBELS.COM

Drawings by Jorge Cabrera, design by Michael Herber, layout by Jessica Herber.

FEB 27, 2005 ✳ 6:30PM DOORS, 7:00PM BOUT ✳ CHEAP SKATE COON RAPIDS 3075 COON RAPIDS BOULEVARD NW ✳ WWW.MNROLLERGIRLS.COM

ATOMIC BOMBSHELLS VS. DAGGER DOLLS GARDA BELTS VS. SILVER BULLETS
✳ ✳ ✳ ✳ ✳ WITH HALF TIME SHOW FEATURING THE SOVIETTES ✳ ✳ ✳ ✳ ✳

By Dan Ibarra, Michael Byzewski and Eric Carlson.

Britt Lundberg-Sax and **Jamie Paul** won the design award at AIGA MN Design Show in 2007 with this Minnesota RollerGirls poster. It was also featured on the cover of Communication Arts 2006 Design Annual, published in HOW International Design Annual and in the 2007 Print Regional Design Annual. For more of their work, head to www.lovelympls.com.

By Britt Lundberg-Sax and Jamie Paul.

"Elegantly Injured," a 2005 poster for the Minnesota RollerGirls, was created by **Imagehaus**. The poster won a HOW Design Annual award and a Print Regional Design Annual award. Imagehaus is on the Web at www.imagehaus.net.

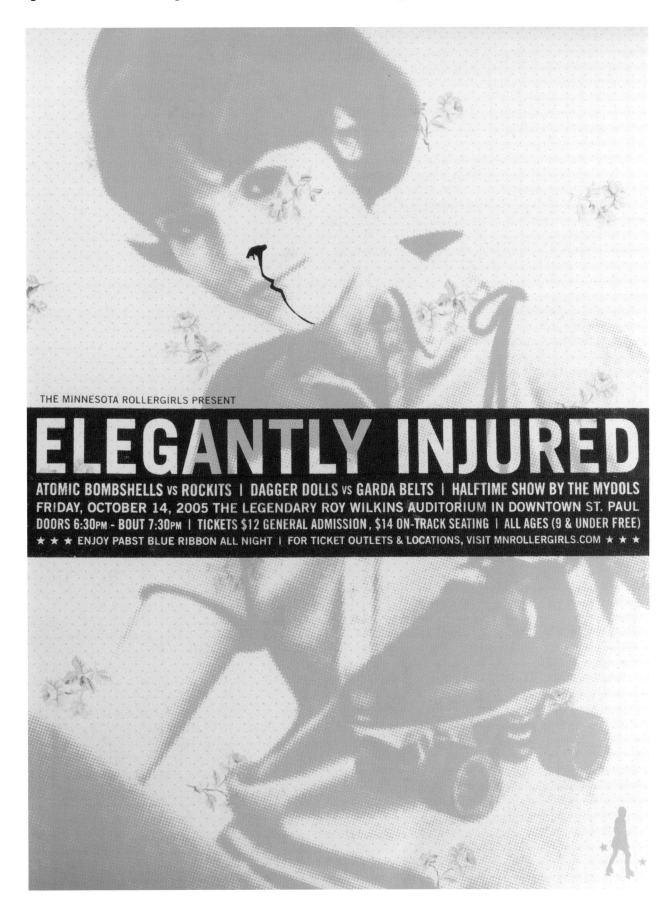

By Imagehaus.

There's an unmistakable cool about a Hatch Show Print poster. Based out of Nashville, Tennessee, the letterpress print shop has been creating promotional materials for stars (think Bill Monroe, Johnny Cash, Hank Williams and more) for decades. Add the Naptown Roller Girls to that ever-growing list.

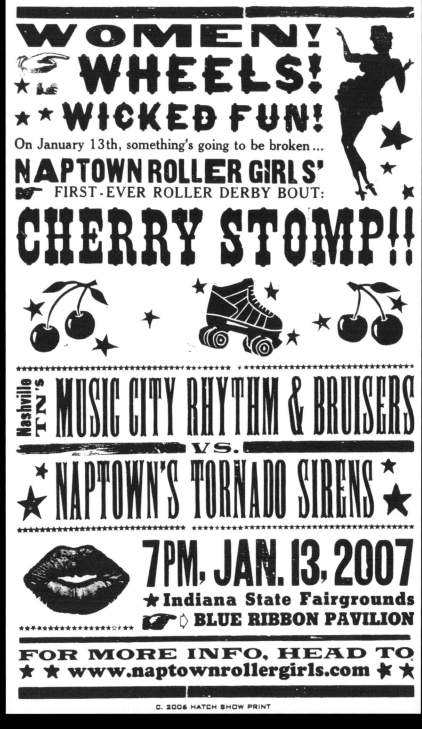

By Hatch Show Print, Nashville, Tenn.

Amy McAdams has been artistically inclined since her early elementary school years in Tipton, Ind. McAdams runs her own design business. She is especially interested in the interplay of typography, colors and composition, and using them to create a whole greater than the sum of its parts. McAdams believes design should be fun, playful and clean all at once. She advocates the liberal use of white space. See her work at www.amymcadams.com. McAdams created the posters as a contract designer for **Well Done Marketing**, a creative company in Indianapolis that has a stake in helping companies and individuals better communicate. Head to www.welldonemarketing.com for more info.

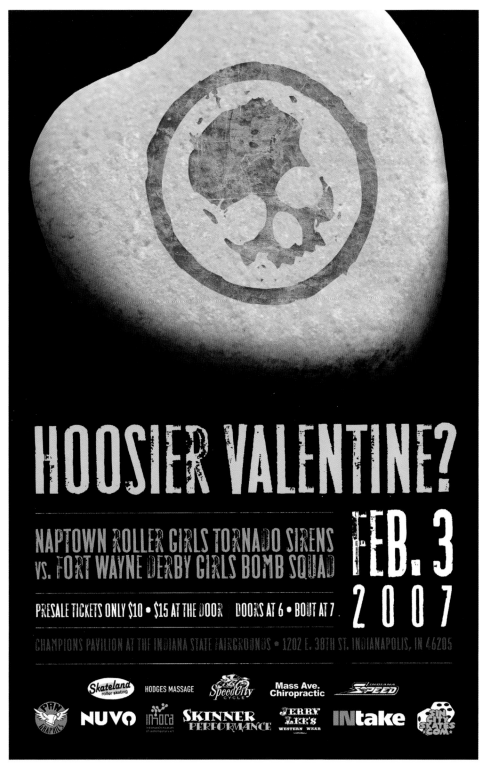

By Amy McAdams and Well Done Marketing.

IF NICE GIRLS FINISH LAST, WE'RE GOING ALL THE WAY.

IT'S REAL. AND THEY'RE SPECTACULAR.

naptownrollergirls.com

From left, Touretta Lynn, Red Rocket, and Lilly Whip.
By Amy McAdams and Well Done Marketing.

Michelle Pemberton and **Ben Roe** are a creative duo who also happen to be hitched. Pemberton is a full-time photographer who dabbles in personal art in her spare time; she's also a former Naptown Roller Girl and current NRG referee. Roe is a full-time graphic artist who also creates a world of wacky online comics at www.roguerobot.com.

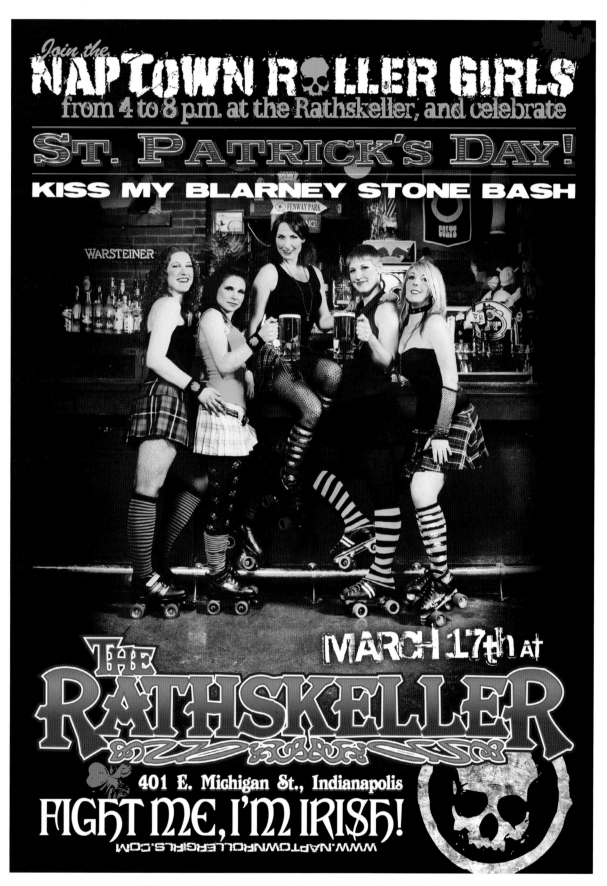

Photography by Michelle Pemberton. Illustration by Ben Roe.

Todd Kennedy says he hates sports—in fact, professional football, he claims, gives him a headache. But he won't miss a roller derby bout, unless he breaks his leg, which forced him to miss one bout during the Naptown Roller Girls first season. When Kennedy, who draws much of his artistic influences from 1970s comic artists and lowbrow art, isn't watching derby or working away the hours at his full-time gig, he's completing commissioned pieces for clients. For more of the man, head to www.myspace.com/todesart.

Arnel Reynon has a long history of creating killer illustrations, and he was kind enough to contribute his talents to the Naptown Roller Girls for the league's Southern Discomfort bout. Reynon currently spends his days working as a publishing director at Sport Graphics in Indianapolis.

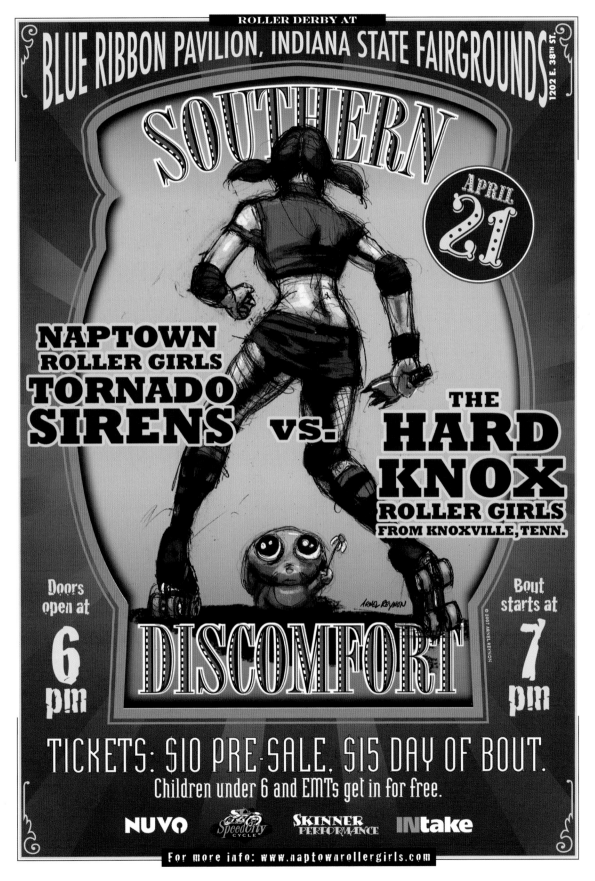

By Arnel Reynon.

Darren Strecker is a freelance illustrator and graphic designer working in Indianapolis. You can see more of his work by visiting his Web portfolio at www.streckergraphics.com.

By Darren Strecker.

Dan Thompson was born and raised in Indianapolis and educated at Herron School of Art and Design. His professional career began as an illustrator and product designer at Fundex Games in Indianapolis, as well as doing several commissioned murals in the city. Currently working for Mediasauce (digital marketing), Thompson's expertise has grown to include a variety of illustration styles, painting and drawing methods, music composition and the occasional voice-over.

As a graphic designer, illustrator, freelancer, full-timer, and all-around visual communicator, **Jason Pitman** is, occasionally, hard to track down. But, according to the Naptown Roller Girls, when you can get the Herron School of Art and Design graduate to serve as your league's designer, you've struck graphic gold. Pitman, who is also lovingly called Pitt Stane, hangs his work at ff4500.com.

By Jason Pitman and Dan Thompson.

The New American Badass
Mark Brocklehurst

A new evolution in women's athletics is taking hold across the United States. It's a sport fueled by adrenaline and dedication. With its roots dating back to the early 20th century, women's flat-track roller derby is making a frantic comeback on a grass-roots and national level. State to state, leagues are sprouting up for the love of the skate. Eight wheels of all-out heart, skill, and devotion set the pace for an exciting and empowering display of athletic skill and prowess in a physically aggressive all-women's sport.

Owned and operated by its members, usually the same women sweating it out on the track, each roller derby league relies on the strong work ethic of its members for its success. The various leagues throughout the country are glued together by the game of roller derby itself, but vary in league formations and styles. There are multiple team leagues and single team leagues. Multiple team leagues usually sport an all-star team from the entirety of the league to challenge teams from outside of their league. There are also single team leagues taking on the best of the best from other leagues. These leagues are often smaller in membership, but work just as hard as or harder than the larger leagues to prepare for competition.

Women's flat-track roller derby is not just a ladies' club. There are many devoted and hard-working men who do whatever is needed within the leagues. These men are often significant others, trainers, skate coaches, or general sports enthusiasts who want to see roller derby succeed. As the head coach and trainer of the Naptown Roller Girls of Indianapolis, Indiana, I am one of those men.

As a coach, I am demanding and austere. I am respectful and impartial, but have no tolerance or patience for disrespect or nonchalance. I have lofty expectations for my team, my league, and myself. I am continually learning and familiarizing myself with new training techniques to benefit my team. I serve as a sounding board for my skaters on a personal level, and I work diligently to make NRG a standout roller derby league. Since NRG is a one-team league, we only play the best of the best from other leagues. The Naptown Roller Girls' competing team is called the Tornado Sirens, and a spot on the team is earned and worn like a badge of pride.

When I started coaching the ladies of NRG, I set personal goals for myself and for the team. I wanted the team to be more conditioned and in shape than any other team in the nation. I wanted the team to be so mentally focused that members would know what to do in any situation on the track, and to be mentally prepared to skate hard and smart for a win. I wanted the team to win more often than not—in a dominating fashion. If a loss does occur, then I hoped it would come at the hands of a superior team and not due to any lapses in mental focus from my team.

I wanted the team to be aggressive, but aggressive as permitted within the rules.

And I am a firm believer that women can train as hard as or harder than men. Breaking down the common gender stereotypes of athletes is a crucial element when trying to establish roller derby as a viable and marketable sport. The ladies of NRG continue to display this notion every time they skate onto a track for a bout or practice. A smart, physically dominating team is a team built on drive, desire and determination, which lead to more wins than losses.

With an athletic background, I saw NRG as a blank canvas coaching-wise. I saw the potential in the ladies: they were able to sustain a high level of physical activity as well as mental fortitude. To me, roller derby is an easy game to understand, but the trick of it is that everything (offense and defense) strategically happens in split seconds and often at the same time. Physical and mental reaction times must be quick. I train my skaters to be mentally and physically prepared for bouts.

I train and push my athletes to the edge. They work extremely hard. Practices are crucial when becoming an elite league. Sometimes it seems that making it through one of my practices is an act of survival for the girls. I push their bodies in several critical ways: through muscle endurance and stamina, overall muscular strength, development of explosive muscle movements, flexibility, resistance training, core strength, spatial awareness, and high levels of sustainable cardiovascular fitness. These are achieved through various drills both in and out of skates. When skaters are at the brink of their physical limit and continue to work, then they are capable mentally of overcoming the rigorous physical output that is required in an actual derby bout.

Roller derby may seem like a simple game on paper, but once the hard skating and hitting start simple goes out the window. That's when peak physical conditioning allows the skater the freedom to visualize and skate a smart bout instead of worrying about how tired they are feeling.

To me, the Naptown Roller Girls offer the community and the roller derby world a source of pride and empowerment. NRG simultaneously smashes gender stereotypes of what athletes should be and continually helps to define a new model for strong women. The Naptown Roller Girls are setting a torrid pace for what a burgeoning women's sport should be. Professional top to bottom, the ladies and men of NRG show how a do-it-yourself attitude coupled with hard work translates into wins on the track, sell-out crowds, and an alternative to other sports that maintains a sense of style and athletic achievement. We are the new American badasses.

Mr. Whip.

By Mike Hrabovsky.

By Mike Hrabovsky.

A BENEFIT FOR THE
NASHVILLE ROLLERGIRLS

FEATURING
THE TRAMPSKIRTS
MARCH 4TH • THE LIPSTICK LOUNGE • 8PM
$5 21+UP • $10 BUYS ALL-YOU-CAN-DRINK BEER

NASHVILLE
ROLLERGIRLS
RECRUITMENT PARTY

7PM TUESDAY JUNE 27th
THE RED DOOR
located at 1816 Division Street

2 for 1 Night—Skaters, Volunteers and Drinkers Wanted

NASHVILLE
ROLLER GIRLS
BENEFIT CAR WASH
SUNDAY, JUNE 24TH 11AM-2PM
$5 MINIMUM DONATION

THE LIPSTICK LOUNGE
1400 WOODLAND ST. - NASHVILLE, TN

By Mike Hrabovsky.

By Mike Hrabovsky.

Kris Notch first became aware of the Omaha Roller Girls in 2006 when the league was looking for a graphic artist to create its posters. It only took a few months, Notch says, for her to fall in love. She soon was a skater playing under the name Ellen DeGenerate. Outside of skating, Notch is an artist by trade, and she's currently training to be a tattoo artist. More of her work is available online at www.krisnotch.deviantart.com.

Tattooist **Mel Judkins** works at Big Brain Tattoo in Omaha, Nebraska, and she brings a background in graphic design, illustration, painting and photography to her work. For more on the artist, hang a left at www.meljudkins.com.

Kris Notch, also known as Ellen DeGenerate.

Logo by Mel Judkins.

Low-Down Lucys Logo by Mel Judkins.

Logo by Kris Notch.

ROLLER DERBY OMAHA

FOR MORE INFO AND OUR CALENDER OF EVENTS VISIT:

OMAHAROLLERGIRLS.ORG

★

JOIN UP
IF YOU THINK YOU
HAVE WHAT IT TAKES,
WE'RE ALWAYS
RECRUITING.

HELP OUT
THERE ARE MANY
WAYS TO SUPPORT
YOUR LOCAL ROLLER
DERBY LEAGUE.

EVENTS ALL YEAR, OFFICIAL SEASON KICKOFF IN JANUARY!
MYSPACE/OMAHAROLLERGIRLS

Magazine ad by Kris Notch.

By Kris Notch.

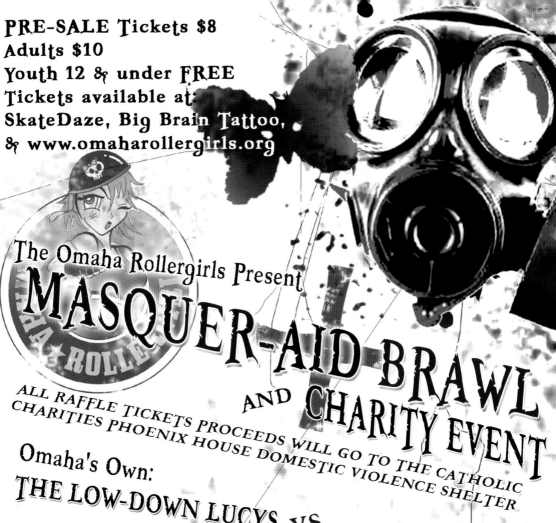

PRE-SALE Tickets $8
Adults $10
Youth 12 & under FREE
Tickets available at:
SkateDaze, Big Brain Tattoo,
& www.omaharollergirls.org

The Omaha Rollergirls Present

MASQUER-AID BRAWL
AND CHARITY EVENT

ALL RAFFLE TICKETS PROCEEDS WILL GO TO THE CATHOLIC
CHARITIES PHOENIX HOUSE DOMESTIC VIOLENCE SHELTER

Omaha's Own:
THE LOW-DOWN LUCYS VS.

VICTORIA'S SECRET SERVICE

Sat, March 24th

DOORS AT 6:30pm
BOUT BEGINS AT 7pm
SKATEDAZE
132ND & 'B'
(Between Center
and L Street)

WWW.OMAHAROLLERGIRLS.ORG

MYSPACE.COM/OMAHAROLLERGIRLS

By Kris Notch.

By Kris Notch.

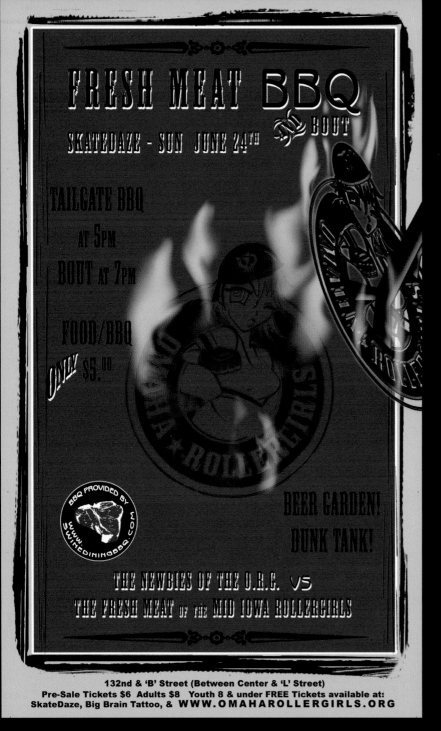

By Kris Notch.

The Pikes Peak Derby Dames league was started during the summer of 2005, and **Amanda Sharpless** (also known as The Swiss Missile) is a skater and resident artist. As a derby girl, Sharpless says she's only had a few injuries: "I was out for the whole first season because I busted my knee. I threw out my lower back, had a couple bloody noses, and thanks to Fanny Fister, I have tiny chips of bone floating under the skin of my left elbow." Sharpless loves to paint and work with ceramics and mixed media; her work can be found at www.myspace.com/holidaysunrise.

Amanda Sharpless (The Swiss Missile) of the Pikes Peak Derby Dames.

Painting by Amanda Sharpless.

Logo by Amanda Sharpless.

Nicholas Baranek, a graphic designer, clothing designer, and a father, dedicates some of his rare moments of spare time to designing artwork for Pikes Peak. Baranek credits the widespread appreciation of hot rod/rockabilly culture for derby's current popularity. "As the demand for custom car / pin-up girl / rock and roll aesthetics develops, there needs to be a sport that also encompasses those core values," he said. "In my designs for roller derby events, I try to use visual cues from the past, and infuse a new modern sensibility into them, using the familiar with the new to create a sort of revisionist visual history and mystique for roller derby to represent." For more from Baranek, head to www.nicholasbaranek.blogspot.com.

By Nicholas Baranek.

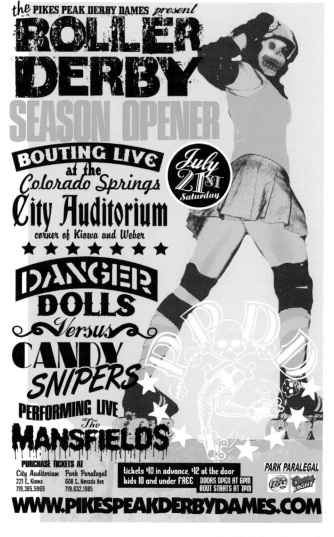

By Nicholas Baranek.

Tattoo artist and graphic designer **Troy Sedlacek** got involved in creating derby art when his wife joined the Pikes Peak league. His wife skates under the moniker Betty Berzerker.

By Troy Sedlacek.

Jake Fahy not only creates art for the Pioneer Valley girls' derby
team in Northampton, Massachusetts, but he also skates for the men's
derby team, The Dirty Dozen. Fahy, who skates as Bazooka Joe #49,
helps run the league, which was established in late 2005.

By Jake Fahy.

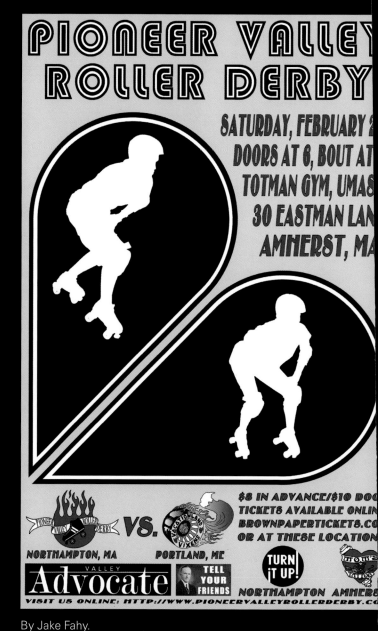

By Jake Fahy.

Dale "Black Dahlia" Rio subscribes to the theory of perpetual motion. She has worked as a freelance photographer and writer for over 10 years. In 2003, when she left the Big Apple for the City of Angels, Rio joined what was then one of a handful of roller derby leagues in the country, the L.A. Derby Dolls. In 2006, she traveled to New Zealand and founded the country's first derby league, the Pirate City Rollers. That year also marked the launch of *Blood & Thunder* magazine, the first roller derby magazine in the U.S., which Rio co-owns and edits. After a short 2007 stint back in New York City, where she skated with the Gotham Girls, Rio relocated to Seattle where she is currently coaching the Jet City Rollergirls. Rio can be reached through www.dalerio.com or www.bloodandthundermag.com.

The Origins of a League
Dale "Black Dahlia" Rio

I had last been to New Zealand in 2004, when I'd started a documentary photo project that I intended to later return to the country to complete. But you know how it is, roller derby got in the way. Skating with the L.A. Derby Dolls had its fits and starts, what with having to find a home for our banked track. When we finally started bouting, I just couldn't tear myself away. But then we lost our warehouse space, and it was taking longer than expected to find another one, so I decided I needed to go. In December 2005, I gave up my apartment, figuring I could find another if I decided to stay in Los Angeles upon my return, and headed to New Zealand for three months.

Some of my kiwi friends knew I was skating. Although they didn't quite know what derby was, they thought it sounded cool. My friend Phili had been interested in giving it a go when I returned, but that never came to pass. She was killed in a car accident before I made it back. Her enthusiasm gave me hope that there was a future for derby in New Zealand, and it was largely because of her that I decided to bring my gear with me when I went back in January 2006. Also because of her, I decided to help get a league going there.

At our first meeting to start the league, I came armed with information. I brought the Derby Dolls' promotional video, Rat City's season one highlights DVD, and tons of handouts pertaining to the business side of things. Looking ahead to the future, I made it clear that if the sport took off, which I fully expected it to, there would be a lot of work involved, since the league was to follow the American skater-owned and -operated mold. Looking back, the girls probably thought I was nuts. I explained to them that committees needed to be formed for sponsorship, fundraising, merchandise, and more—and all for a sport that didn't exist yet! But they were game, so we tracked down the last skate rink in Auckland to rent quads and started going to open-skate sessions.

Although New Zealand has a large speed skating community, roller skating in general isn't popular, so many of the girls had to learn skating basics first. In those early stages, people came and went. Some were curious but decided skating wasn't for them. Some were interested but were put off by the potential for injury. Some stuck it out. They saw it as a challenge. Those girls became the core of the Pirate City Rollers.

By the time I left in April, we had secured one private practice session at Skateland per week. But with such limited time to practice and a lot of learning to be done, I'd already decided to come back later in the year. I left Pieces of Hate and Bonnie Blaggard, two skaters who showed both leadership and skate skills, in charge of holding down the fort. I provided them with two-months' worth of "lesson plans" and returned to the States.

In the U.S., it's easy to take for granted how much people want to be involved in derby. Bouting venues get sold out, leagues have waiting lists for new skaters, and there are armies of volunteers who help out. But in a country like New Zealand, which has never seen the sport before, it's hard to explain how derby has grown so quickly to people who haven't witnessed it first-hand. I imagine it can be hard for the girls who are struggling today to envision themselves bouting in front of thousands of fans within a few years' time. I'm sure it can seem as if all the hard work may never pay off. At times I thought I was the only one who could imagine the future of the sport in New Zealand, solely because I had the advantage of having watched it develop in the States, but I could tell that some of the others got it, too.

During my absence, the Pirate City Rollers held it together through drive and determination. When I returned in September 2006, I was amazed to see how much the girls had improved. They had developed a good rapport with Skateland's manager, who I think viewed us as a very odd novelty, and the rink's learn-to-skate and speed skating classes were now open to the Pirates. It was obvious that several had taken advantage of Skateland's offerings. I was excited to see that even outside of the U.S., people could still be bitten by the roller derby bug!

For the next three months, we went into full-on derby mode. Everyone worked really hard, both on and off the track. The Pirates had been able to add a second official practice to the schedule, and people were getting together outside of practice to skate, either at open-skate sessions or anywhere they discovered smooth surfaces in town. With relatively small numbers, we had league-wide meetings every week, where committee members reported to the group. We printed out the WFTDA rules, and the league hashed them over, clarifying points that seemed unclear, and adapted the rules to suit the Pirates' needs.

The challenge of ordering skates was overcome when the league hooked up with Sin City Skates. (Another thing we Americans take for granted is the ease with which we can procure gear. In New Zealand, it's virtually impossible to find good quad skates, so they have to be ordered from overseas. With customs fees and shipping charges, ordering skates means a definite commitment.) Getting helmets proved to be a challenge, though, as it ended up taking months' worth of phone calls and faxes to finally receive the shipment. Needless to say, this held up scrimmaging, and with what seemed like ages of drills under their belts, the girls were itching to try out their skills in actual game play.

It had been our goal to hold a public bout before I left in December, but with the delays, it seemed like that might not happen after all. When we talked about having a season, or even a one-off public bout, some of the girls seemed skeptical about it: Who would actually pay to come see us play? Again, with the advantage of having seen derby grow in the States, I thought, "Oh, just you wait and see!"

We agreed on opening up one of our scrimmage practices to friends and family and decided on a date two days before I was scheduled to fly out of Auckland. We had also been invited to Wellington, New Zealand's capitol, the weekend before the open practice to do some demos at Ladyfest, an international event celebrating art and music by women. A bunch of us piled into a van and made the trek to spread the good word of derby. What an awesome trip that was! We did a daytime demo on a makeshift track down by the waterfront and one at night on the street outside the club that was hosting the festival's shows. We had a blast, and there was interest from some of the locals about starting a league there.

Everyone who came to watch the Pirate's open practice loved it. The skaters who had been nervous were bolstered by the positive comments they received, and with that first, small showing, the Pirate City Rollers were on their way. The girls decided to have a short series of exhibition bouts in March 2007 in order to raise public awareness and recruit new skaters, and although I wasn't there to witness it first-hand, by all reports, the bouts were huge successes. The crowd loved the game, and there was a sharp increase in new recruits. The media also picked up on the new sport, and the league has since been inundated with requests. A handful of leagues have also sprung up in nearby Australia, so the Pirates don't have to feel so separated from derby's mainland any more. Hopefully they'll soon have competition in the South Seas!

It kills me to have to hear of their progress from the other side of the planet, but I know that one day I'll make it back to Auckland and skate proudly with the Pirates. What the league has accomplished is absolutely amazing: developing their skills and their understanding of the game in isolation and introducing a completely new sport to their country.

As an aside, I have the admit that all the league's successes—past, present, and future—are bittersweet to me, because I know that if Phili were alive today, she'd be cheering us on the loudest, if not skating right beside us. Phili was my inspiration and driving force from the get-go; I envisioned helping to create an organization that she'd enjoy being a part of. Everything I've done with and for them has been with her in mind; she is constantly in my thoughts when I'm in Auckland, and when I'm skating with the Pirates, I wish she were here to join in on the fun.

Dale Rio (red-and-black striped shirt in the front row) with the Pirate City Rollers.

Anna Belle Wong skates as Wonton Destruction for the Pirate City Rollers, a league established in 2006. Wong heads up the Pirates' art department and works by day designing print ads, in-store signage and direct mail.

Anna Belle Wong as Wonton Destruction. Photo by Matt Lowden.

By Anna Belle Wong.

By Anna Belle Wong.

Scott Loke Grigg is an "artist by trade, hobby, specialty, amusement, weakness and whatever other category I can be placed in," he said. "I am a lifetime artist." His life's work can be found at scottgrigg.com.

Scott Loke Grigg.

By Scott Loke Grigg.

135

Michael Grigg owns Royal Magnet, a company that has produced Web sites for bands like The White Stripes, The Raconteurs, The Shins and more. The company's work can be seen at www.royalmagnet.com.

By Michael Grigg.

Pris Toff is a jammer and blocker for the Throttle Rockets, one of the Rat City teams.

Hand-illustrated poster by Throttle Rocket Pris Toff.

136

When **Jamie Burton** isn't working, he says he's at home painting for one gallery show or another or making silkscreen posters. Burton says he was drawn to derby because "he liked the retro feel of bringing back an old sport. I really dig the styles of the girls; they all have their own look and tend to look a lot like the girls I usually draw." Check out Burton's work at www.jamieburton.com.

Jamie Burton.

By Jamie Burton.

By Jamie Burton.

Pat Moriarity is a professional illustrator and cartoonist whose work includes CD cover art for the Boss Martians and Von Zippers, contributions to Nickelodeon and National Geographic Kids magazine and more. His work hangs out at www.patmoriarity.com.

Pat Moriarity.

By Pat Moriarity.

Art is a trade and a hobby to **Jeremy Beson** and **Jon Estrella**, members of Stateless, an artist collective in Seattle. For more on their work, visit www.sttlss.com.

By Jeremy Beson and Jon Estrella, members of the artist collective Stateless.

By Chris Honeywell.

Chris Honeywell says he's a part-time artist and full-time designer who was drawn to roller derby because there were "women roller skating and kicking ass." His art can be found at www.chrishoneywell.com.

Augie Pagan says he was asked to do a poster for the Rat City league, and he jumped at the chance. "Who wouldn't want to draw roller derby girls?" he said. Pagan, a full-time artist, hangs his work at www.augiepagan.com.

By Augie Pagan.

140

Krysztof Nemeth says he's a pin-up artist, and he was first asked to draw a logo for the Rat City gals. Nemeth was soon creating league posters, limited-edition art and logos for leagues and teams all over the country. What drew him to it, he says, is how "badass" the sport it. "It's the spectator sport for the D.I.Y. generation," he said. "It's a rolling, rumbling pit of strong and sexy sisterhood.

"I've utilized roller derby as something of a role model for my young daughter," he said. "She sees strong women doing their own thing, working as a team, putting their soul into the spectacle. She sees a creative bunch of girls using their strength and talent in a way that's not exploitative or co-opted. It's totally unique to each girl, each team, each league. What a great example for a young girl to get to move forward in life with!" Nemeth's work can be found at www.charm-school.com or www.myspace/krysztof.

By Krysztof Nemeth.

By Krysztof Nemeth.

141

Jay Barber, an illustrator and animator, works for a video game effects company. More of Barber's work can be found at www.myspace.com/jayrolfbarber.

By Jay Barber.

Graphic designer **Kristi Simmons** skates as Ruby ROX for the Wicked Pussycats, one of the teams in the Renegade Rollergirls league. Her artwork is housed at www.ksimmonsdesign.com.

By Kristi Simmons.

By Tori Justino (Ginger Kamikaze). Art direction by Kristi Simmons. Photography by Lance Hardy.

By Kristi Simmons. Photography by Lance Hardy.

By Kristi Simmons. Photography by Lance Hardy.

By Kristi Simmons.

By Kristi Simmons.

By Kristi Simmons. Photography by Lance Hardy.

By Kristi Simmons. Photography by Lance Hardy.

By Kristi Simmons.

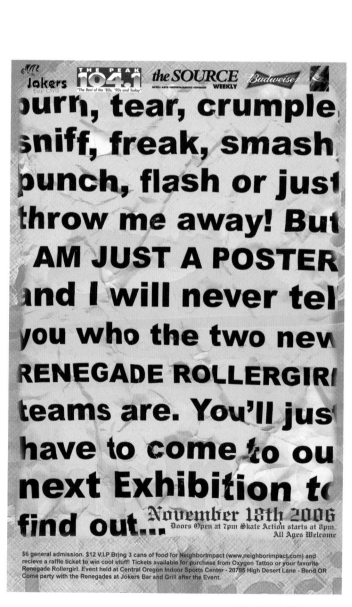

By Kristi Simmons.

Jay Vollmar got involved with derby when his girlfriend joined the Rocky Mountain Rollergirls in 2004. He says other than making posters and logos for the league, his involvement with derby includes frequently letting his home be "overrun by visiting teams looking for a place to crash and by league meetings where I try to steal their beer and cupcakes." Vollmar's art hangs out at www.jayvollmar.com.

Logo by Jay Vollmar.

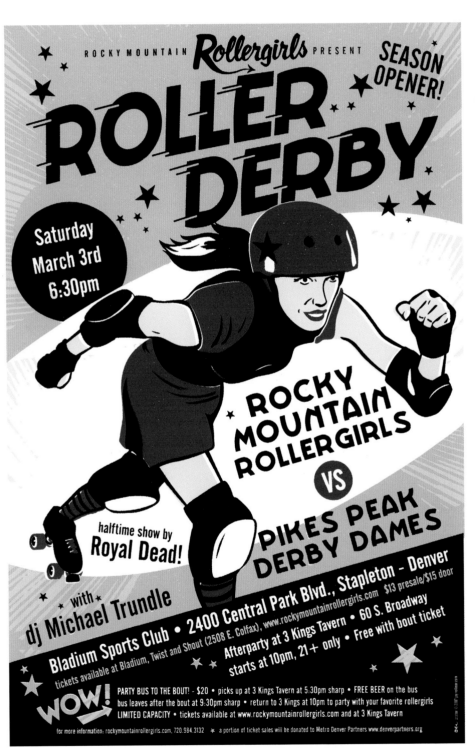

By Jay Vollmar.

By Jay Vollmar.

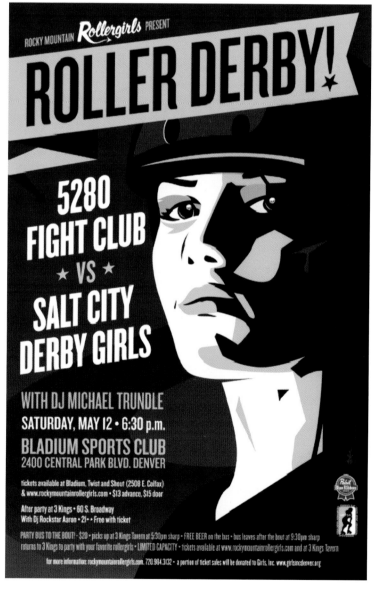

By Jay Vollmar.

149

By Jay Vollmar.

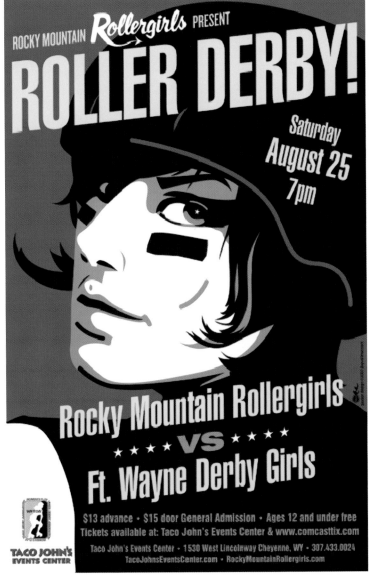

By Jay Vollmar.

By Jay Vollmar.

By Jay Vollmar.

Rob Walkowiak started working in the commercial sign business in 1997, but his creative side lead him to creating Skull Lords Design, through which he landed work creating fliers for club concerts and promotions. "Working in the sign business provides little in the creativity department," he said. "A majority of customers who come through the door are usually scared to try anything different or new. Most always want the same thing that they saw down the road, so a good outlet for me is, for the most part, band fliers. You can come up with the most off-the-wall style for a concert flier and people love it. It's probably my favorite thing to do."

To feed that love, Walkowiak eventually took on more work with show promoters, bands and the local roller derby league, The Rogue Rollergirls. Walkowiak says he began designing logos, buttons, banners, fliers, and posters for the league, while his wife Sarah decided to join the sport as a skater. Walkowiak's work can be found at www.skulllords.com.

"I think it's fantastic that roller derby is on the map again. It's an awesome sport that definitely deserves its time in the spotlight. And all these girls work their asses off just for the love of the game."
Rob Walkowiak

Rob Walkowiak of Skull Lords Design.

For the Reedy River Roller Girls. By Rob Walkowiak.

For the Rogue Rollergirls. By Rob Walkowiak.

By Rob Walkowiak.

By Rob Walkowiak.

By Rob Walkowiak.

By Rob Walkowiak.

The Magazine: *Blood & Thunder*
Dale "Black Dahlia" Rio
www.bloodand thunder mag.com

Soon after I became fully entrenched in roller derby, I realized that it was completely suited for a print publication. The world of derby encompasses far more than the game itself; it's a sub/pop-culture phenomenon that includes the off-track (often fascinating) lives of the skaters, the fashion aspect of the sport, bands and other performers who entertain at derby events, the businesses that sponsor leagues, the artists who make bout posters, the cities that are home to derby leagues, and so on. With an entire "scene" having developed around roller derby, with such a far-reaching appeal, it seemed to me that not only skaters, but anyone who was interested in popular culture would be interested in a magazine that celebrated this sport.

I first had the idea of starting *Blood & Thunder* in 2004. It's probably for the best that my master plans didn't come to fruition then, because even though those of us who were involved had the sneaking suspicion that the sport would grow exponentially, only a handful of leagues existed at that point.

Having worked for several publications as a freelance photographer and writer, I had some early offers of assistance and potential partnership from people I knew from "the industry." But none of them felt quite right. First and foremost, I envisioned the magazine being run with the same "skater-owned and -operated" ethos that the leagues operate on. The people who had approached me had the lure of financial backers and ties to existing publishers, but they didn't have an intimate knowledge of (and love for) the sport—even if they did have an appreciation for it.

One of these early "partners" suggested I change the name because with the word "blood" in the title, the magazine probably wouldn't be picked up by Wal-Mart. Although her insight was appreciated, I couldn't even imagine coming up with a Wal-Mart-acceptable alternative. Another person recommended I tap into a stable of his photographer friends. Not only was I personally rankled, being a professional photographer myself, but most of the people he suggested were middle-aged men who specialized in fetish photography. They may have been talented, successful photographers, but I knew in my heart that there was plenty of talent from within the derby family to choose from, and the last thing I wanted to invite into that family was a team of droolers. (Derby already draws enough of those!)

In early 2006, Robin Graves, a friend with whom I had skated in L.A., and I decided to start putting out a pocket-sized burlesque magazine called *Shimmy*, after Robin quit her tedious day job in search of something more fulfilling. With

155

her experience in design and my photography background, we made the perfect team.

Around that time, all my outside options, as far as making *Blood & Thunder* a reality, seemed to run out, and self-publishing appeared to be the only route available. Robin and I created Black Graves Media, (a combo of both of our skate names), an umbrella company that oversaw both magazines, and we enlisted the design expertise of Danny Echevarria, the husband of L.A. Derby Doll Razorslut. And *Blood & Thunder* came to be.

We put out a call for contributors from within the derby community and were lucky enough to hear back from professionals of all sorts, (writers, photographers, designers, and illustrators), who were willing to contribute their talents to our endeavor, all for the love of derby. In the beginning, I had to come up with most of the content myself, but now I get so many pitches for article ideas, it's almost impossible to keep up with them all. Without the dedication and selflessness of these contributors, the magazine wouldn't exist, and there's no way to thank them enough for the work they do.

The two hardest things about putting out *Blood & Thunder* have been the financial and business aspects of self-publishing. With no experience in the behind-the-scenes operations of the publishing business, Robin and I have had to learn it all as we've gone along. What an eye-opener! With just the two of us doing all the office work, we have had to play the roles of ad wrangler, subscription service, merchandiser, shipper/receiver, accountant, and more, along with our official roles of designer and editor/contributor.

I like the idea that the magazine has developed like the sport of roller derby itself—with the people involved having to figure everything out on their own, often through trial and error. It exemplifies my goal of running the magazine in a way that parallels the sport. Luckily, we've encountered many patient roller girls who understand that it's a huge undertaking that we've brought upon ourselves and not everything will run smoothly.

On occasion, we have received unnecessarily snarky feedback, which I take very personally. It makes me want to invite these people to experience the all-nighters and drained bank accounts that Robin and I have suffered in order to produce *Blood & Thunder*. I naively like to think that all roller girls would have a modicum of understanding, since they all must have gone through similar growing pains with the formation of their leagues. But some seem to think that an omniscient magazine guru handed Robin and me a fail-safe, how-to manual when we decided to jump in head-first. In reality, we're just two women producing two magazines during our off-time from motherhood (for Robin), and a full-time job, freelance work, and skating (for me).

Oh, yeah ... the drained bank accounts. When we started *Blood & Thunder*, we started with a circulation of 5000 copies at full-color production. Based on the ever-growing numbers of roller derby leagues, I figured we would have no problem at all attracting enough advertisers and subscribers to finance the magazine. But I wasn't exactly correct. A year later, most of the printing expenses are still being paid out of pocket. It's also a vicious cycle. With more money coming in, more money goes out. With more money, we could hire a subscription service to take that responsibility off of our hands. With more money, we could increase our page count and improve our paper stock, resulting in a slicker magazine that would attract more advertisers. With more money, we could advertise *Blood & Thunder* in other magazines and outlets and increase our subscription base. And so the cycle goes.

Even though there are days when I question whether it's worth the anxiety and frustration, the ulcers, the constant shell game I play with my credit cards, it all seems worth it when I look at the four existing issues to date and can see, quite apparently, the progress and improvements we've made along the way. It's worth it when I see the look on a skater's face when she sees her story, photo, or name in print. It's worth it when a nine year-old fan tells her favorite skater she saw her in a copy of *Blood & Thunder*. It's worth it when a reader says that (s)he really related to an editorial that I wrote, or that we "took it up a notch" with our most recent issue.

We started with nothing but my stubborn vision of what I imagined a roller derby magazine to look like: something that would do right by the skaters. Now we have a publication that is slowly, but surely, growing. Just like derby. And, just as many leagues are making the move from dusty warehouses and smelly skate rinks into sports arenas, some day *Blood & Thunder* will be a beautiful magazine, over 100 pages in length, with immaculately reproduced photos on thick, luxurious paper stock, and it will be available at every newsstand in the country! Check, make that the world!

Viva la derby!

Sin City Rollergirls

Ivanna S. Pankin, who many also know as Denise Grimes, owns and operates the Sin City Skates roller derby gear shop and skates for Arizona Roller Derby in Phoenix, Arizona. She founded Arizona Roller Derby in 2003, skated in the first-ever inter-league game against Texas Rollergirls in 2004, and moved to Las Vegas in 2005, where she captained the Sin City Rollergirls for two years before heading back home to Arizona. She maintains ties to Vegas, however, to more easily plan RollerCon, the annual roller derby convention every summer. Her Web site is www.sincityskates.com.

Ivanna S. Pankin. Photo by Robert Folliard

By Denise Grimes.

Poster design by Denise Grimes (Ivanna S.
Pankin). Illustration by Brianne Young (Pirate).

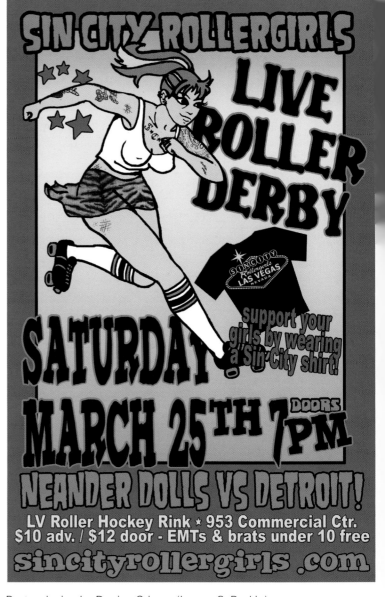

Poster design by Denise Grimes (Ivanna S. Pankin).
Illustration by Brianne Young (Pirate).

By Denise Grimes.

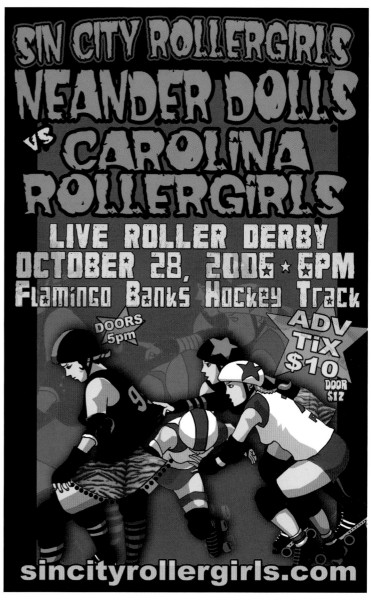

By Denise Grimes.

By Denise Grimes.

By Denise Grimes.

Texas Rollergirls

Christina Pocaressi, also known as Voodoo Doll, has been skating with the Texas Rollergirls for more than five years, and she says she's been lucky enough "to watch this sport evolve from a bar joke into a revolution." A proud pivot for her team, the Hotrod Honeys, Pocaressi is a part of the original group of girls in Austin, Texas who got the sport rolling.

She also got her start with art in a most unusual way: "Am I an artist by trade? Not even," she said. "On a fluke, I was elected art director of the league, and they needed posters and logos right away. I bought a used computer from Goodwill and stared at the screen wondering what I'd gotten myself into. I didn't even know how to use Photoshop. After three days of banging my head against the keyboard I just got the hang of it and the designs came pouring out: Posters, postcards, bumper stickers."

Apparently people liked what she did. "Word got out and I started getting hired to design everything from corporate logos to Web sites to cheesecake boxes," she said. "I have no technical ability; I just go into Mad Scientist mode and people seem to like it." Pocaressi can be reached through www.tabutoys.com.

"Have I been injured? I'm walking around with someone else's Achilles tendon in my knee. I measure my time in roller derby not by dates but by a series of injuries. 2003 was the year of the severed PCL. (The year) 2004 was the hematoma that looked like my embedded twin. 2005 was Satan's own parking-garage road rash. 2006 was my introduction to sciatica. When you play a full-contact sport eventually something has got to give. Show me the girl who's played longer than two years and never gotten hurt. (So I can choke her.)"
Voodoo Doll #29

PHOTO: MIKE OSBORNE

Voodoo Doll Christina Pocaressi of the Texas Rollergirls
Photo by Mike Osborne.

By Christina Pocaressi.

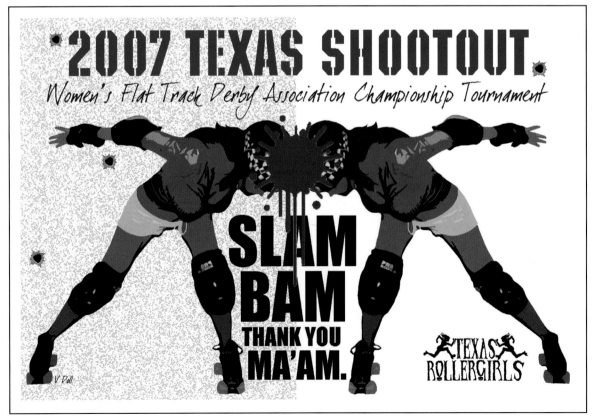

By Christina Pocaressi.

By Christina Pocaressi.

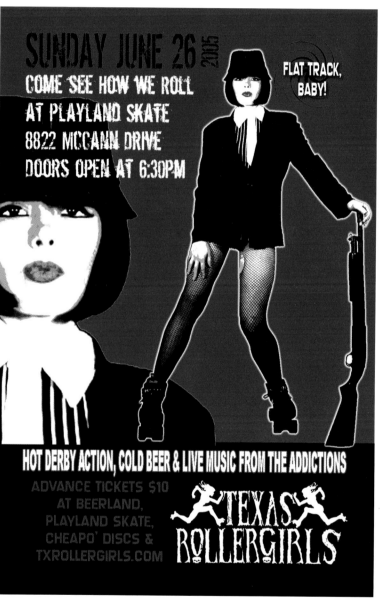

By Christina Pocaressi.

By Christina Pocaressi.

Tucson Roller Derby

Since 1997, **Bradley Zimmerman** has been creating posters and artwork in Pittsburgh and the Tucson/Phoenix areas under the names Adrenachrome-Design and Poptastic.biz. Concentrating primarily on work promoting concerts and events, he has appeared in various publications and rock poster books. Zimmerman became involved with roller derby via his significant other, and says he has been taken advantage of on a regular basis under ludicrous deadlines for the past four years. In return, Zimmerman reports positive results in getting his lady friend interested in ice hockey, which he pitched to her as "roller derby with weapons."

Zimmerman's injuries, thanks to roller derby: "Bumps/bruises/muscle-pulls from bout set-up and tear-down, perpetually frazzled nerves, 'derby tinnitus'—a constant ear inflammation suffered by roller girl boyfriends who have to be a constant sounding board for derby-talk."

Why derby rocks, according to Zimmerman: "In Tucson, the inevitable self-esteem boosts have encouraged participants to make some pretty incredible changes in their lives—from starting their own businesses, to ending bad relationships, to taking classes for things they discovered they had a knack for after having responsibility thrust upon them by the league. Obviously the health benefits are amazing—it's much easier to motivate yourself to hit the rink with your team than some gym by yourself. Derby does change lives."

By Bradley Zimmerman.

By Bradley Zimmerman.

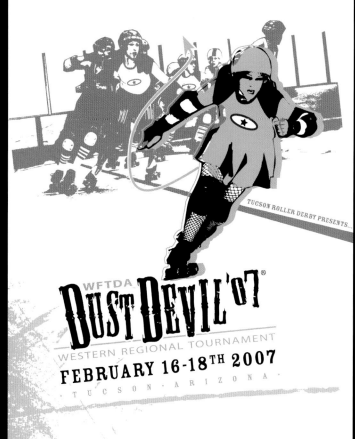

By Bradley Zimmerman.

By Bradley Zimmerman.

By Bradley Zimmerman.

By Bradley Zimmerman.

By Martin Cimek.

By Martin Cimek.

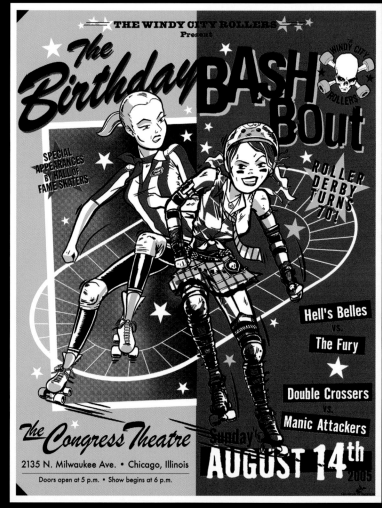

By Martin Cimek.

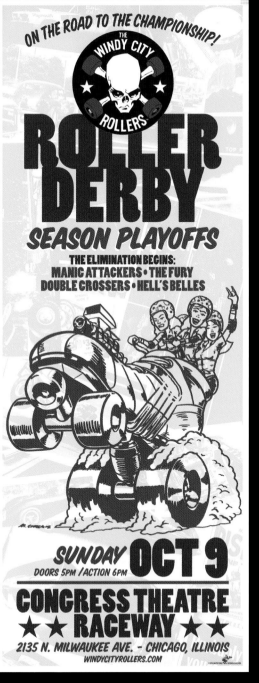

By Martin Cimek.

By Martin Cimek.

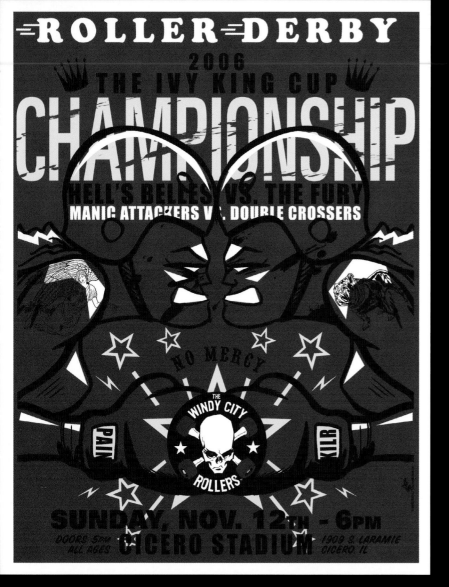

By Martin Cimek.

Eric Persson has been producing artwork on some level his entire life. He started painting as a student at Kansas State University; these days, his artistic subjects vary from figurative forms to abstracts and landscapes—always with a vivid color palate and expressionistic brush stroke. Persson began working on this series of derby girls, after he became a fan of the sport, which he says he finds to be a "combination of athleticism and art." Persson's work, which has been included in several corporate collections including The Kansas City Sports Commission, WIN for KC and The National Center for Drug Free Sport, can be found at www.ericjpersson.com.

By Eric Persson.

By Eric Persson.

The Players

Jammer (star on helmet)

Pivot (stripe on helmet)

Blocker   **Pivot**

The Rules

Scoring Pivots set the pace of the pack. The Jammers start behind the Blocker Pack and must skate through it to score. Points are counted starting with the second pass through the pack. 1 point for each opposing blocker passed.

Strategy The first Jammer through the Pack while staying in bounds is dubbed Lead Jammer.

The Lead Jammer can call off the Jam (hands on hips) to keep the other team from scoring.

Allowed Body checking from the front or side.

Penalties Punching, tripping, grabbing, shoving, biting. The worst offenders must face judgement of the Die Master!

175

By Eric Persson.

Chapter 4
Girls, Girls, Girls!

Strawberry Jam (left) and Lilly Whip. Photo by Michelle Pemberton.

Apocalyptica, L.A. Derby Dolls.
Photo by Dale Rio.

Charlie Trouble, Pirate City Rollers. Photo by Dale Rio.

Blazin' Ace, Naptown Roller Girls. Photo by Tom Klubens and Michelle Pemberton.

Ana Slays Ya (back) and Joan of Dark, Naptown
Roller Girls. Photo by Michelle Pemberton.

Lil' Deville, Pirate City Rollers. Photo by Dale Rio.

Jane Ire (left) and Slammy Faye, Naptown Roller Girls. Photo by Greg Perez.

Charlie Trouble, Pirate City Rollers. Photo by Dale Rio.

Varla Vendetta, Windy City Rollers. Photo by Dale Rio.

Attack of the 50-Feet Women: Sweet C (left) and the author, Touretta Lynn, Naptown Roller Girls. Also featuring Naptown announcers Dill Hero and Brownie Hero. Photo by Michelle Pemberton. Illustration by Ben Roe.

General Lee Feisty, Lonestar Roller-girls. Photo by Dale Rio.

Sin Lizzie, Naptown Roller Girls. Photo by Tom Klubens and Greg Perez.

Rollita, Bay Area Derby (BAD) Girls.
Photo by Dale Rio.

4 Leaf Cleaver (left) and Mother Russia, Naptown Roller Girls. Photos by Tom Klubens and Michelle Pemberton.

Blazin' Ace, Naptown Roller Girls. Photo by
Tom Klubens and Michelle Pemberton.

Buckshot Betsy, Texas Rollergirls.
Photo by Dale Rio.

Jen X, Naptown Roller Girls. Photo by Tom
Klubens and Michelle Pemberton.

Smackie Onassis, Naptown Roller Girls.
Photo by Tom Klubens and Marc Lebryk.

Red Rocket, Naptown Roller Girls. Photo by Tom Klubens and Marc Lebryk.

Strobe Lightning, Rat City Rollergirls. Photo by Dale Rio.

Dirty Little Secret, Rat City Rollergirls. Photo by Dale Rio.

From left: Hot Luvin', Ruby Scar-let, Quick Sand, Mr. Whip, Arch Angel, Fin Addict, Cereal Killer, Malady, CR Wrecks, Kitiara and Shadi Layne, Naptown Roller Girls. Photo by Tom Klubens and Michelle Pemberton.

Cherry Chainsaw, Lonestar Rollergirls. Photo by Dale Rio.

J. Roller and Diane Beatin', Naptown Roller Girls. Photo by Tom Klubens and Michelle Pemberton.

Strawberry Jam, Naptown Roller Girls. Photo by Michelle Pemberton.

Chapter 5
The Fans and Their Fearless Leader

Renee "Nay" Sweany, Fearless Leader
Naptown Roller Girls [unofficial] Fan Club
www.nrgfanclub.com

Life in roller derby takes a lot of turns. Left turns. Here's a short story of a derby season with a few *whips*, a couple elbows to the ribs, a *tush push* or two, one *rock star* (noun) and one *rock star* (verb).

Renee Sweany and Christopher West, both NRG[U]FC steering committee members.

Naptown Roller Girls [unofficial] Fan Club in full effect.

Turn 1

I went to my first bout in January, not knowing what to expect. It was the first bout of the season—the Naptown Roller Girls also didn't know what to expect. We both were pleasantly surprised.

My usual energetic self transformed into a derby freak. With more than 2000 people, it was standing-room only. I didn't understand a thing, but I stood and I yelled. My friends say I was louder than the blaring music. I don't believe that. I could hear the music just fine.

After the bout, my friends went to my place for a post-party. A tradition began.

Turn 2

My second derby, I just knew I had to sit in the suicide seats, which is the area sectioned off for those daring enough to sit on the floor and brave the possibility that skaters will land in our laps. We arrived early and camped out between turns 3 and 4 next to a cute little photographer. Throughout the bout, my pal and I debated photo-boy's straightness. Apparently my chant-leading, boisterous way intrigued him, too. My tipsy invitation to attend our post-party was indulged. And that's how I met Nate.

Between 2 and 3

Lots of great things happen between turns 2 and 3. Jammers squeeze through the pack. Pivots and blockers nudge out the competition. Sometimes both skates leaving the ground. Fans welcome roller girls into the suicide seats. Beers get spilled. And derby fans fall for one another.

Nate and I were nearly inseparable. Our enthusiasm for how we met led to perhaps one of my best ideas yet—a Naptown Roller Girls fan club. We didn't even think twice—we just got to work.

Not knowing at all what this fan club could mean to fans and roller girls alike, we chose the name Naptown Roller Girls [unofficial] Fan Club (NRG[u]FC). We knew we needed a Web site, which led to ideas of roller girl interviews, fan interviews, drink recipes named after roller girls (I already had one from the first bout, thanks to Busty Sanchez and some tasty banana rum), photos … the options were limitless. As we threw ourselves into the fan club, we threw ourselves into a crazy love affair.

Being fans of the NRG became a favorite hobby. I idolized them the way a teenage girl adores a boy band. The best part, the feeling became mutual. As our list of fans grew, the roller girls became our number one fans.

With the fan club also came an amazing group of old, new, unexpected and completely welcomed friends ready to spray paint bandanas, make banners, glue photo boards, form a jug band without any jugs—and wash it all back with a Pitt Stane (another league-inspired drink). We call ourselves the steering committee—a rather official name for such an unofficial group—and we all have titles: Fearless Leader, Band Director, Sharpee Tattoo Artist, Community [reach around] Relations, to name a few.

We cheered, we hugged after victories, we high-fived after losses. A peak moment was the pep rally before a home bout in the parking lot of the fairgrounds. The NRG[u]FC brought together young and old for "photo as a Naptown Roller Girl," banner signing, corn hole and good old-fashioned derby camaraderie. The pep rally was also the first opportunity for members to show their NRG[u]FC membership cards for a fan bandana.

Turn 3

When the home season ended and the dreaded derby hiatus began, I jokingly asked Nate if he thought our relationship could survive without derby. The NRG[u]FC took a little break from the part-time job of Web site updating and craft-making. We attended away bouts with the same verve as those at home. Our roller girl sightings were fewer, but just as exciting. The very best part is that our fan/roller girl relationship had grown into friendship.

If you'll recall, Nate and I met between [the literal] turns 3 and 4, and we're now between turns 3 and 4 [figuratively] in my story. What more appropriate time for the sweethearts of the derby to skate in different directions. As the NRG travel season came to an end, so did Nay and Nate. Face it, derby love is just too good to be true. But the love of derby is untouchable.

Logos by Mitch O'Connell.

Mitch O'Connell is a beloved hanger-on of the lowbrow art movement. His work has been featured in magazines like *Newsweek* and *Playboy* and on CDs by bands such as The Supersuckers and Less Than Jake, and it has been exhibited in a variety of galleries from New York to Berlin. His tattoo designs are also a fixture on the walls of tattoo shops around the world. To learn more about the O'Connell, visit www.mitchoconnell.com.

189

Index of Featured Leagues

Index of Artists